All Aboard!
FOR GLACIER

THE GREAT NORTHERN RAILWAY
AND GLACIER NATIONAL PARK

BY C. W. GUTHRIE

FARCOUNTRY
PRESS

TITLE PAGE: *From the Great Northern Railway brochure* The Call of the Mountains.
COURTESY K. ROSS TOOLE ARCHIVES, UNIVERSITY OF MONTANA, MISSOULA

FRONT COVER: *Illustration from a magazine ad.*
COURTESY BURLINGTON-NORTHERN-SANTA FE RAILWAY

BACK COVER: *Page art from a Glacier National Park mountaineering booklet.*
COURTESY JOHN CHASE COLLECTION AND BURLINGTON-NORTHERN-SANTA FE RAILWAY

Acknowledgments

This book contains numerous historical photographs obtained from universities, historical societies, national park archives, and private collections. While acquiring these photographs it has been my great pleasure to work with Wendy Hill of the Glacier Natural History Association; Teresa Hamann, Donna McCrea, Jennifer Rusk, and Mark Fritch at the University of Montana; Craig Wright and Steve Nielsen of the Minnesota Historical Society; Dierdra Shaw and Somer Treat of the Glacier National Park archives; Brian Shovers of the Montana Historical Society; Walter Sayre of the Stumptown Historical Society; and Scott Tanner and Lindsay Korst of the Great Northern Historical Society. I am especially indebted to Frances Liebig and Ted Soldowski for use of their albums, books, and papers; and John Chase, Bruce Thisted, Stephen Prince, and Lauri Wilson for permitting me to use their private photograph collections in this book. John Chase provides an impressive display of historic photographs at Glacier National Park every year. They can be viewed at Glacier Park Lodge, the station at East Glacier, and the Many Glacier Hotel. Bruce Thisted and Lauri Wilson provided the Winold Reiss art from their collections, and Stephen Prince provided the photographs of the Belton station. It takes a lot of work to bring a book together from a jumble of text and pictures, and no one does it better than the staff at Farcountry Press. It has been a pleasure working with Bob Smith, Jessica Solberg, Kathy Springmeyer, and freelance editor Barbara Fifer. I appreciate your help. Thank you all.

ISBN 1-56037-276-1

© 2004 Farcountry Press

For more information on Farcountry Press books, write Farcountry Press, P.O. Box 5630, Helena, MT 59604, call (800) 821-3874, or visit www.farcountrypress.com

Created, produced, and designed in the United States of America.
Printed in Korea.

TABLE OF CONTENTS

Great Northern Railway calendar with Winold Reiss painting of Scalping Woman (note misspelling of Scalping on calendar).
COURTESY LAURI WILSON

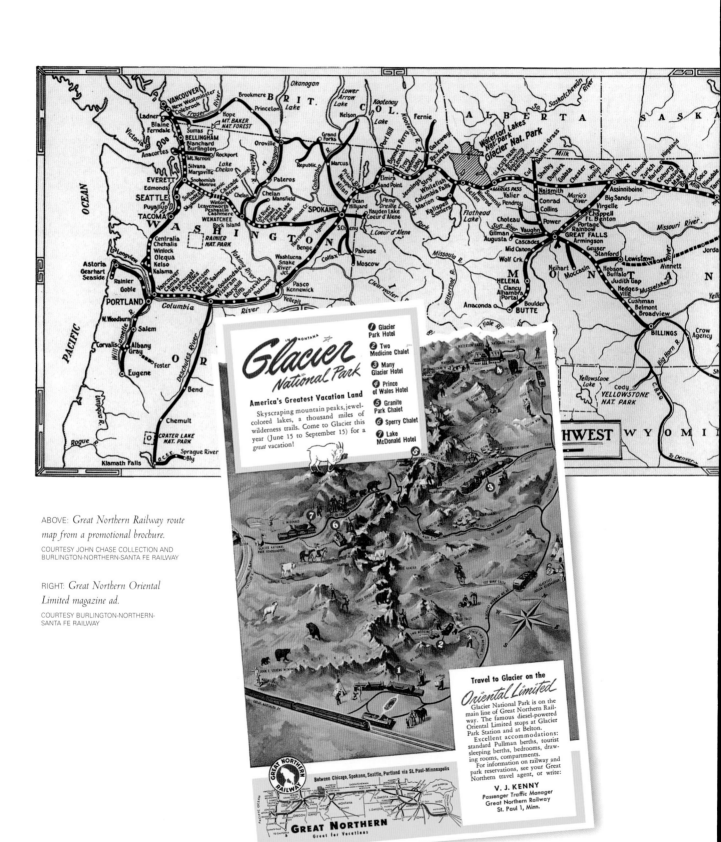

ABOVE: *Great Northern Railway route map from a promotional brochure.*
COURTESY JOHN CHASE COLLECTION AND BURLINGTON-NORTHERN-SANTA FE RAILWAY

RIGHT: *Great Northern Oriental Limited magazine ad.*
COURTESY BURLINGTON-NORTHERN-SANTA FE RAILWAY

CHAPTER I

Over Valley, Plain, and Peak

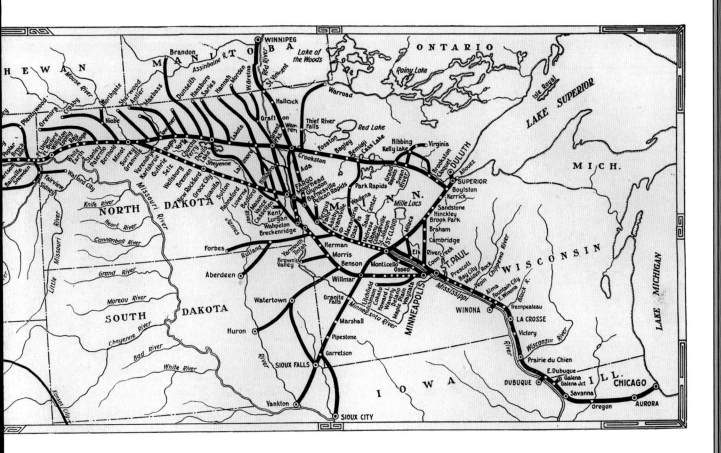

"Before the days of the railway, it was a journey of as many months as it now takes days to reach the Pacific Coast. Then it was a perilous trip with dangers besetting the wagon trains on every side. Now the railway cars, with the iron horse in front, his cyclopean eye shining out into the darkness hurry along against the wind or rain without dismay, leaping the rivers and climbing the mountains, the traveler enjoying the while all the comforts of home."

—*Valley, Plain & Peak*, Great Northern booklet, 1894

The main line of the Great Northern Railway stretched 1,816 miles from St. Paul, Minnesota, to Seattle, Washington, through the prairies and plains of North Dakota and Montana, over the rugged Rocky Mountains, and through the splendid canyons of the Cascades to the Western Sea. But it was the sixty-mile stretch of rail from east of the Rockies through Marias Pass and along the Middle Fork of the Flathead River—bordering the grandeur

and breathtaking scenery of Glacier National Park—that the Great Northern showcased to lure people from all over the world to the conductor's call for "All aboard." Glacier and the Great Northern Railway became synonymous in the early twentieth century.

As their tracks were being laid across the top of the country, agents of the Great Northern Railway were busy launching a series of promotional projects to bring immigrants to the northwest and lead development of the vast

RIGHT: *Great Northern train highballing through Marias Pass.*

COURTESY MINNESOTA HISTORICAL SOCIETY, GREAT NORTHERN RECORD COLLECTION

INSET: *Magazine ad.*

COURTESY JOHN CHASE COLLECTION AND BURLINGTON-NORTHERN-SANTA FE RAILWAY

Many Glacier Hotel on Swiftcurrent Lake

Welcome Back to Glorious Glacier Park!

This summer Glacier National Park reopens its picturesque hotels and chalets.

Somewhere West of Worry, U.S.A.

I'm headin' west of Worry, U.S.A.
I've said good-bye to Hurry every day,
Now my only real ambition
Is to be in the condition
Of having nothing else to do but play.

• So head for Montana's Glorious Glacier Park and Waterton Lakes Park, Alberta—where American and Canadian Rockies meet. This is magnificent vacation country with cozy hotels and chalets, with unforgettable launch trips on lovely alpine lakes and sightseeing motor coach rides on spectacular scenic highways. Superb trout fishing, hikes, horseback riding, golf. On any Western trip, travel via Great Northern Railway one way at least. It costs no more and the transcontinental Empire Builder stops at both rail entrances to Glacier Park.

Write to A. J. Dickinson, Passenger Traffic Manager, Great Northern Railway, St. Paul 1, Minnesota, for more information about vacations and stop-off tours in Glacier National Park.

See America — First the West
Plan Your Postwar Vacation around Glacier-Waterton Parks
• No matter where you plan to go in the West, include a stop-off at Glorious Glacier Park. Inquire about these four popular vacations.
Glacier Park and California
Glacier Park and Canadian Rockies
Glacier Park and Pacific Northwest
Glacier, Yellowstone and Dude Ranches

Route of the Empire Builder
BETWEEN CHICAGO, ST. PAUL, MINNEAPOLIS, SPOKANE, SEATTLE, TACOMA, PORTLAND AND VANCOUVER, B. C.

GREAT NORTHERN RAILWAY

natural resources along the route from St. Paul, Minnesota, to the Pacific coast. The railroad took a similar role in developing Glacier into a world-class tourist destination. Its Great Northern Company built campgrounds, hotels, and Swiss-style chalets throughout the area, promoting fishing, boating, hiking, and riding, and joined George Bird Grinnell and Lyman Sperry in leading the campaign to make a national park. As early as 1894, Great Northern's advertising campaign invited visitors to take the train to the "Alpine grandeur" of Lake McDonald, amid the "Swiss Alps of America." The advertising campaigns would continue through the years, reflecting the times and capturing the mood of the country with such slogans as "The Greatest Care-killing Scenery on the Continent," "America's Greatest Vacation Land," and "See America First."

The mountain goats of the Rockies inspired the Great Northern logo, and Great Northern was so identified with Glacier that the Great Northern goat became the symbol of both the railroad and Glacier National Park.

We will never know what Glacier would be like today if the Great Northern had not come along. Perhaps it would still be a part of the Blackfeet Indian Reservation, and its lakes, streams, mountains, and wildlife still a favored hunting ground. Perhaps this land of glacier-sawn peaks, peerless mountains, rushing falls, colorful gorges,

hanging valleys, and magnificent lakes would have been protected as a national park without the railroad's help. Perhaps individual settlers and entrepreneurs would have provided the tourist facilities that were built by the Great Northern. Perhaps, instead of creating a park in 1910 and preserving Glacier's natural resources, the nation may have chosen to ruthlessly exploit them in the American rush for wealth. We'll never know, and second guessing history does little good. What is certain is that the manmade history of Glacier National Park is inextricably tied to the Great Northern Railway. So, too, is Great Northern history tied to the call of Glacier's valleys, plains, and peaks.

BOTTOM: *Great Northern Railway dining car menu.*
COURTESY JOHN CHASE COLLECTION AND BURLINGTON-NORTHERN-SANTA FE RAILWAY

BELOW: *Great Northern 1914 logo.*
COURTESY GLACIER NATIONAL PARK ARCHIVES

5807. Blackfeet Indian Encampment, St. Mary Lake, Glacier National Park, Montana. On Main Line Great Northern Railway See America First

ABOVE: *The first train over the Great Northern Line.*
COURTESY STUMPTOWN HISTORICAL SOCIETY, WHITEFISH, MT

LEFT: *Postcard promoting the Great Northern Line.*
COURTESY COLLECTION OF ROBERT SMITH

CHAPTER 2

Pardon Me Boys, but It's the Great Northern

The story of the nation's fifth transcontinental railroad, the Great Northern, is a tale of entrepreneurial genius, grit, and greed. Its founder, James J. Hill, was like the locomotives he sent west: a one-eyed, self-propelled engine of unstoppable force. He made the country from the Great Lakes to Puget Sound and Oregon his empire. He is credited with "desolating Minnesota, populating the Dakotas, making Montana a state and stealing Puget Sound." Loved and despised, respected and feared, he would become the greatest railroad baron of them all.

Henry Villard of the Northern Pacific, and the railroad barons of the Union Pacific, the Southern Pacific, and the Atchison, Topeka & Santa Fe were predicting disaster for James J. Hill and his Great Northern Railway, calling it "Hill's Folly." These transcontinental railroaders had received vast land grants from the government that fetched millions of dollars, and had chosen routes along paths traveled by immigrants headed for California goldfields and Oregon farmlands. The Northern Pacific was already running trains along the northern tier of the United States in the country Hill chose for his railroad and—even with its huge land grants and government loans—the NP was in deep financial trouble. Congress thought the nation had as many transcontinental railroads as it needed and was still smarting from the financial troubles of the Northern Pacific. They were in no mood to subsidize another railroad. Hill built his railroad without government land grants and chose a route across the top of the nation through uninhabited prairies and wilderness. It did, indeed, seem to be folly.

But Hill was a man of extraordinary vision, enormous energy, and stalwart determination. When he decided to do something, it was as good as done! While most of his contemporaries were certain his railroad was a fool's venture, Hill was just as sure he could make this far northern

route profitable. His closest competitor, the Northern Pacific, was poorly built over steep grades and around numerous curves. It had cost too much to build and

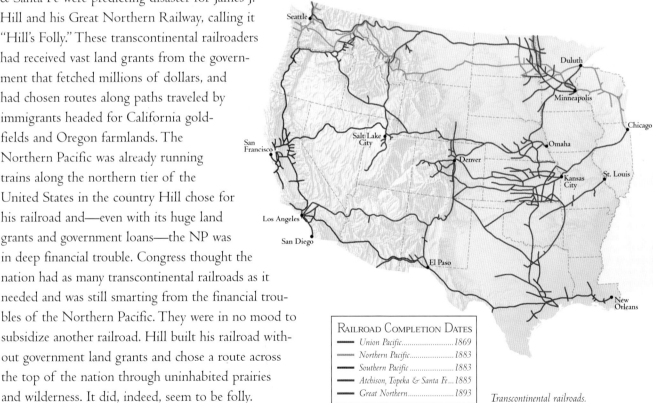

Railroad Completion Dates	
Union Pacific	1869
Northern Pacific	1883
Southern Pacific	1883
Atchison, Topeka & Santa Fe	1885
Great Northern	1893

Transcontinental railroads.

was in continuous financial trouble. Hill would put his railroad over a better route and "build it right." Before he retired and turned his railroad business over to his son Louis in 1907, James J. Hill would build the best constructed, most financially sound transcontinental railroad in the nation, populate the northwest, take control of the Northern Pacific, and reign over a third of all the railroads in the West. The man and his life would be summed up as "The Empire Builder."

THE EMPIRE BUILDER

James J. Hill, like most of the railroad barons, had humble beginnings. He was born in the Canadian bush in 1838 to a Scots-Irish family that farmed fifty acres near the settlement of Rockwood, Ontario. A childhood accident with an arrow blinded him in one eye but it did not impair him or the man that he would become. He learned reading, writing, arithmetic, geography, English, Latin, Greek, and geometry at an academy run by a college-educated English Quaker, receiving an extraordinary education for his time and circumstance. By age ten, James had acquired a passion for reading that would last his lifetime. At home he had read the Bible, the dictionary, the works of Shakespeare, and the poems of Robert Burns. At the academy in Rockwood were many more books to choose from. He read them all. He had a particular interest in the biographies of explorers and great mili-

James J. Hill, 1912. COURTESY MINNESOTA HISTORICAL SOCIETY

tary leaders. Men who dared to venture into the unknown and men who conquered nations and built empires were his heroes: Marco Polo, Napoleon, Genghis Khan, Alexander the Great.

During his fourth year at Rockwood Academy, James' father died. At fourteen he became head of the family. He found work in a grocery store in the nearby settlement of Guelph and the family moved into town. He clerked at the store for four years, saving what money he could, reading whenever he had time, and dreaming of going to far-off places. In 1856, when he was not quite eighteen, Hill set out for Philadelphia, where he planned to get work on a ship going to the Orient. He ran out of money near Syracuse, New York, worked awhile for a farmer then went on to New York City, then to Philadelphia. But the opportunity to ship out from Philadelphia to the Orient never came.

Undaunted, he decided to make his way to San Francisco or Portland, where he hoped he

Tourists enjoying the scenery from a Great Northern Oriental Limited passenger train observation deck.

COURTESY GLACIER NATIONAL PARK ARCHIVES AND BURLINGTON-NORTHERN-SANTA FE RAILWAY

could work for his passage on one of the ships sailing from the Pacific ports. He worked his way from Philadelphia to St. Paul, where each spring a brigade of fur trappers left for the Rocky Mountain trapping grounds. He hoped to join them on their journey westward but he arrived a week too late. His dream of going to the Orient would have to wait and he seemed to set it aside, although eventually Hill extended his empire across the Pacific to Asia.

When young Hill stepped ashore at St. Paul in the late 1850s, the town was a hive of activity, a hustling, bustling center of trade. Keelboats, sidewheelers, and sternwheelers paddled up and down the Mississippi bringing goods and supplies in from Dubuque, St. Louis, and New Orleans to be loaded onto oxcarts and taken overland to trading posts and settlements springing up on the new frontier. Riverboat bells clanged and warning whistles sounded as the boats pulled up and departed the levee. Captains shouted orders and roustabouts loaded and unloaded cargo.

Five thousand people hustled along the muddy streets next to the levee. Bullwhackers drove their wooden-wheeled oxcarts through muck-rutted roads to unload furs bound for the eastern and European markets, then loaded up supplies destined for the Red River of the North and the trading posts of Canada. Land speculators wheeled-and-dealed, homesteaders wandered in and out trading for supplies, and ambitious merchants were hastily building shops and stores, hotels and saloons. St. Paul was in its first great boom. Twelve hours after James arrived he was hired as a clerk for J. W. Bass & Company, agents for the Dubuque & St. Paul Packet Company's line of river steamboats. St. Paul would be his home until he died in 1916.

Hill was not a tall man, even for his time. He had short thick legs, a long torso, and such massive shoulders and thick, sinewy arms he projected a sense of tremendous strength. His intense gray eyes revealed a sharp mind, boundless energy, and a fiercely competitive nature.

View of St. Paul from the Mississippi River, 1894.

VALLEY, PLAIN & PEAK: SCENES ALONG THE LINE OF THE GREAT NORTHERN, GREAT NORTHERN 1894 BOOKLET; COURTESY K. ROSS TOOLE ARCHIVES, UNIVERSITY OF MONTANA, MISSOULA

ST. PAUL, the capital of Minnesota, stands on a series of terraces overlooking the Mississippi River at the head of navigation ; is the focus of immense railway systems extending in every direction, the center of an enormous wholesale and retail trade, and contains numerous large manufacturing concerns. The Mission of St. Paul was founded in 1841 ; in 1846 a post office was established ; the following year the town of St. Paul was platted. Beautiful in situation and surroundings, and blest with an invigorating climate, this northern capital has drawn to its gates an enterprising and cultivated population, in 1894 numbering 175,000.

"I do not see why St. Paul should not become one of the notably most beautiful cities in the world. * * * Summit Avenue is literally a street of palaces. * * * It is not easy to recall a street and a view anywhere finer than this, and this is only one of the streets conspicuous for handsome houses."—*Charles Dudley Warner in Harper's Magazine.*

14

Even in his youth he was a man to be reckoned with, one determined to make his mark.

Young Hill drank some, gambled some, and was quick to get into two-fisted brawls. He generally had a good time on the levee. Nothing, however, kept him from taking care of business. It was on this Mississippi riverfront that James Hill honed his natural entrepreneurial instincts to razor sharpness. He

1862 St. Paul & Pacific Railroad time table.

COURTESY JOHN CHASE COLLECTION AND BURLINGTON-NORTHERN-SANTA FE RAILWAY

understood the forces of politics and the dynamics of trade, and he would use or create them to forge his empire.

Hill was astute with figures and in a very short time his employers allowed him to fix freight and passenger rates. He learned everything there was to know about the Mississippi packet business—routes, distances, times of arrival and departure of boats, stages, and oxcart trains of all the companies on the riverfront. He quickly discovered that the packet business was a cutthroat operation, and he viewed that aspect of commerce as an invigorating challenge to be met and bested. Before long he was running the business for J. W. Bass & Company.

When the Civil War started in 1860, he tried to enlist but was refused because of his blind eye. During the war years he continued to run the packet business and ventured into a number of sidelines. By the end of the war he had set himself up as a forwarding agent in charge of the Northwestern Packet Company. This company had traffic arrangements with the Chicago, Milwaukee & St. Paul Railroad, and the Illinois Central. A year later Hill had managed his way into becoming agent for the new and ambitiously named St. Paul & Pacific Railroad Company, whose ten miles of tracks ran from St. Paul to St. Anthony—the latter town soon to become Minneapolis. Hill built a warehouse near the depot to eliminate the costs of drayage from dock to rail. He proposed to the St. Paul & Pacific Railroad that he should supply the fuel for their locomotives. Hill provided the wood for a time but he considered wood a poor fuel for locomotives. He leased vast deposits of coal in Iowa and convinced the railroad that coal was better. Then, with his good eye on the future, he took in a financial partner and organized Hill, Griggs & Company. Hill's new company operated a freighting, merchandising, and warehouse business and held the monopoly on the coal business in St. Paul. By 1866, Hill, at age

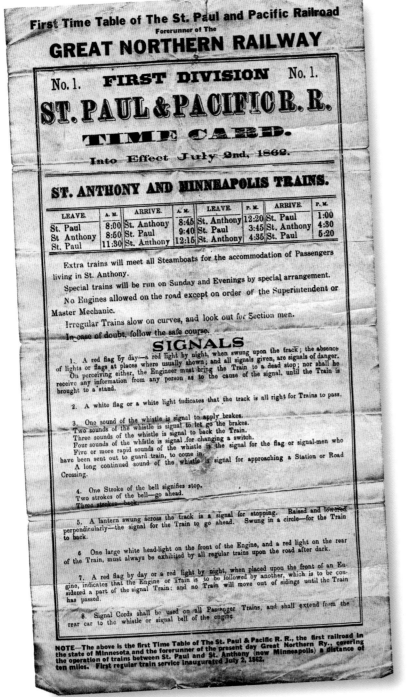

First Time Table of The St. Paul and Pacific Railroad
Forerunner of The
GREAT NORTHERN RAILWAY
No. 1. FIRST DIVISION No. 1.
ST. PAUL & PACIFIC R. R.
TIME CARD.
Into Effect July 2nd, 1862.
ST. ANTHONY AND MINNEAPOLIS TRAINS.

LEAVE.	A. M.	ARRIVE.	A. M.	LEAVE.	P. M.	ARRIVE.	P. M.
St. Paul	8:00	St. Anthony	8:45	St. Anthony	12:20	St. Paul	1:00
St Anthony	8:50	St. Paul	9:40	St. Paul	3:45	St. Anthony	4:30
St. Paul	11:30	St. Anthony	12:15	St. Anthony	4:35	St. Paul	5:20

Extra trains will meet all Steamboats for the accommodation of Passengers living in St. Anthony.

Special trains will be run on Sunday and Evenings by special arrangement.

No Engines allowed on the road except on order of the Superintendent or Master Mechanic.

Irregular Trains slow on curves, and look out for Section men.

In case of doubt, follow the safe course.

SIGNALS

1. A red flag by day—a red light by night, when swung upon the track; the absence of lights or flags at places where usually shown; and all signals given, are signals of danger. On perceiving either, the Engineer must bring the Train to a dead stop; nor shall he receive any information from any person as to the cause of the signal, until the Train is brought to a stand.

2. A white flag or a white light indicates that the track is all right for Trains to pass.

3. One sound of the whistle is signal to apply brakes.
Two sounds of the whistle is signal to let go the brakes.
Three sounds of the whistle is signal to back the Train.
Four sounds of the whistle is signal for changing a switch.
Five or more rapid sounds of the whistle is the signal for the flag or signal-men who have been sent out to guard train, to come in.
A long continued sound of the whistle is signal for approaching a Station or Road Crossing.

4. One Stroke of the bell signifies stop.
Two strokes of the bell—go ahead.
Three strokes—back.

5. A lantern swung across the track is a signal for stopping. Raised and lowered perpendicularly—the signal for the Train to go ahead. Swung in a circle—for the Train to back.

6. One large white head-light on the front of the Engine, and a red light on the rear of the Train, must always be exhibited by all regular trains upon the road after dark.

7. A red flag by day or a red light by night, when placed upon the front of an Engine, indicates that the Engine or Train is to be followed by another, which is to be considered a part of the signal Train; and no Train will move out of sidings until the Train has passed.

8. Signal Cords shall be used on all Passenger Trains, and shall extend from the rear car to the whistle or signal bell of the engine.

NOTE—The above is the first Time Table of The St. Paul & Pacific R. R., the first railroad in the state of Minnesota and the forerunner of the present day Great Northern Ry., covering the operation of trains between St. Paul and St. Anthony (now Minneapolis) a distance of ten miles. First regular train service inaugurated July 2, 1862.

twenty-eight, was a prominent, respected businessman and the most successful forwarding agent in St. Paul.

Hill's reputation as a man who got things done would lead to his next venture and form the foundation of his fortune. Norman Kittson, a Canadian fur trader, had come to St. Paul in the 1830s. Kittson traded on his own and served several terms in the Minnesota legislature representing the independent fur traders of the Pembina district, the region bordering Canada. In the 1860s he became the St. Paul agent for the Hudson's Bay Company, and in 1866 was elected mayor of St. Paul. Hill's friendship with Kittson would impact the course of Hill's life and pit him into battle against the Hudson's Bay Company.

The British charted Hudson's Bay Company had dominated the fur trade on the continent since 1670, at one time controlling fully one-third of present-day Canadian territory. By 1821 the company controlled trading from the boundary of Labrador to the Pacific Ocean, and from the lower reaches of the Mackenzie River to the American passes over the Rocky Mountains. Hudson's Bay traded vigorously throughout the west and north and southward from the Missouri River to San Francisco Bay. In 1857, a Parliamentary Inquiry decided that what is now southern Alberta, Saskatchewan, and Manitoba was suitable

for settlement and ceded it to Canada. It was the beginning of the end of the Hudson's Bay foothold on trading in North America. Independent trappers were invading its historic trapping grounds, and Scottish sheepmen and farmers were settling the fertile lands of the Red River basin in Manitoba.

Hudson's Bay made a last-ditch effort to hold on to its trade dominance by opening a quick route for its men into and out of the Red River basin to the fast-growing Minnesota towns on the Mississippi. The best route was overland from St. Paul to the Red River of the North, which forms the border between

Glacier National Park brochure.

ABOVE: *Steamer* Selkirk *on the Red River, circa 1872.*
COURTESY MINNESOTA HISTORICAL SOCIETY

RIGHT: *Hudson Bay Company seal on the grounds of Lower Fort Garry.*
COURTESY MINNESOTA HISTORICAL SOCIETY

BELOW: *Hudson's Bay Fort at Pembina.*
COURTESY MINNESOTA HISTORICAL SOCIETY

Minnesota and North Dakota then flows north into the Red River basin in Manitoba and on to Lake Winnipeg. Hudson's Bay bought an old Mississippi River boat, tore it down, carted it to the Red River near present-day Fargo, reassembled it, christened it *The Pioneer,* and launched it to move Hudson's Bay's men, supplies, and trade goods between Minnesota and their Fort Garry (now Winnipeg, Manitoba) post.

Norman Kittson was once an independent trapper and trader and, even in his present position as agent for Hudson's Bay, he was covertly loyal to the independents he had represented in the legislature. He suggested to James Hill that it might be a profitable venture if Hill could find a way to haul the independents and their supplies to and from Minnesota and Dakota and the trapping and farming regions of Manitoba. Hill jumped on the idea. He was still affiliated with the St. Paul & Pacific Railroad. The railroad laid track northwest to St. Cloud, Minnesota, shortening the distance by oxcart by about seventy miles. At St. Cloud, passengers and freight were loaded onto oxcart and dogsled stage and freight teams and taken to Fort Abercrombie, near the headwaters of the Red River of the North, and to other landings along the river. At the landings they could board Hudson's Bay Company steamers for the trip to Fort Garry. Hill's shorter, quicker route across Minnesota made the business immensely profitable.

The Hudson's Bay Company had the only steamer navigating the Red River and it carried only the Company's goods. The next step in Hill's scheme to transport independent trappers was to challenge the Company's monopoly on the Red River. In 1870 he sent men to Fort Abercrombie to build flatboats and cut oak and plank for steamboats. Then he set out for Fort Garry by stage and dogsled to take a look at the country. During the following year he made several trips to the Red River Valley. Despite the danger and brutal hardships of trekking through the wilderness, Hill would explore every foot of the country, every hill, every pass, every waterway. Personally getting to know the country he was about to conquer was a pattern that Hill followed when he started his businesses in St. Paul and he would do the same again when he began planning his transcontinental railroad.

In 1871, Hill's steamship *Selkirk* boldly pulled up to the levee at the fast-growing town of Winnipeg, as an astonished crowd of trappers, merchants, and settlers looked on. The Hill steamship lines now provided freight and passenger service between Minnesota and Winnipeg. Hill also had another surprise for the Hudson's Bay Company. He dug up a long-ignored American law that required all goods passing through American territory intended for Canada to be bonded in the United States customs. Hill persuaded the American government to enforce the law. The oxcart brigades and the Hudson's Bay Company's steamer had not complied with the law, so for a short time Hill had a monopoly while Hudson's Bay Company sorted out its legal issues. The company transferred their steamer to their agent in St. Paul, Norman Kittson, an American citizen who promptly bonded the boat.

In their game of one-upmanship, the Hudson's Bay Company now announced it would accept freight from the independents. Hill countered by cutting freight and passenger rates, and wheeling and dealing merchants, trappers, and traders into using his steamer and flatboats. The competition was fierce and neither company was gaining. Finally, Hill met with Norman Kittson and Donald Smith, the head of the Hudson's Bay Company. The three formed the Red River Transportation Company under Kittson. Rates on the Red River went up and the new company earned a net profit of eighty percent the first year.

Although the Red River Transportation Company would be the foundation of his

fortune, Hill decided that overland by rail was his next domain to conquer. He needed a railroad. The opportunity came during the panic of 1873. Philadelphia banker Jay Cooke's bank failed when he tried to raise $100 million to finance the completion of the Northern Pacific Railroad. When that bank failed it set off a nationwide crash. The St. Paul & Pacific, already in financial trouble, went bankrupt. Hill went to Norman Kittson with a plan to make the St. Paul & Pacific profitable again. The two of them went to Donald Smith of the Hudson's Bay Company, who contacted George Stephen, president of the Bank of Montreal. They eventually added John S. Barnes of the J. S. Kennedy Bank to

Great Northern Railway hiking brochure.
COURTESY JOHN CHASE COLLECTION AND BURLINGTON-NORTHERN-SANTA FE RAILWAY

RIGHT: *Magazine ad.*
COURTESY JOHN CHASE
COLLECTION AND BURLINGTON-
NORTHERN-SANTA FE RAILWAY

BOTTOM: *Glacier National
Park brochure.*
COURTESY JOHN CHASE
COLLECTION AND BURLINGTON-
NORTHERN-SANTA FE RAILWAY

the group. The horse-trading and legal maneuvering went on for about five years and the deal finally went through in March 1878. The five had bought the financially crippled St. Paul & Pacific for about twenty percent of its value.

At age forty, Hill's next great challenge was to turn the St. Paul & Pacific into a profitable railroad. The St. Paul & Pacific did have a land grant, good only in Minnesota, that entitled the railroad to ten acres for every mile of track laid. However, the grant required that track to Alexandria be laid by December 1 of the same year that Hill took control.

Another threat loomed just to the south of his planned railroad. The Northern Pacific was making plans to run a line connecting to the Canadian railroad, which is exactly what Hill had in mind. It was crucial to hold on to the Minnesota land grant but just as important to his railroad to develop Manitoba and outfox the Northern Pacific for Canadian business. Hill would do both. He bluffed the Northern Pacific into agreeing not to compete with his railroad for Manitoba business. Then, in late May, he set out to lay track to Alexandria and on to the international border to connect with the Canadian Pacific to Winnipeg by year's end.

He bargained for rails, rolling stock, locomotives, and hundreds of laborers. He directed the construction, ramrodded the work, and drove his men through the blistering heat of summer and bitter cold of winter to lay one mile of track a day. When a crew quit, he wired St. Paul to send him more men, and hired thugs to guard each door to discourage any notions of quitting before reaching the job. Hill walked the grade, watched the men, called them by their first names, and kept a frugal eye on materials. When snow piled high and slowed work, Hill got out of his private car and started shoveling, sending some of the frostbitten, weary men in to drink coffee and warm up while he shoveled. He was alternately brutal or considerate, but he kept men working. Hill had trains running from St. Paul to

Winnipeg by January 1879. That May he reorganized his railroad into the St. Paul, Minneapolis & Manitoba.

Hill received over three million acres of Minnesota land for completing the rail line on time, and sold it as homesteads to the numerous and eager Norwegian and Swedish immigrants arriving in the United States, bringing in over $13 million for the railroad. Good harvest seasons for the next several years brought more business to his railroad.

Hill was already planning his route to the Pacific but he spent the next few years ensuring the financial soundness of his railroad, sorting out problems of the Canadian Pacific (he was a board member), and vigorously promoting development of Manitoba and the American portion of the Red River Valley, which in turn would bring business to his railroad. Hill's campaign was successful. Forty thousand immigrants were plowing fields, planting crops, and building farms and towns on the Canadian and American sides of the Red River Valley by 1881.

When Hill was satisfied that everything was going well in the north, he headed west to take on Dakota. Although Hill's competition in the northwest—Henry Villard's Northern Pacific Railroad—was hastily laying track east to west and west to east to become the second transcontinental railroad, Hill appeared to be in no great hurry. Hill's tracks west were slowly being laid across Dakota when the Northern Pacific transcontinental line from Duluth to Tacoma was completed in 1883.

TOP RIGHT: *Newspaper cartoon of Hill planning his railway lines.*
COURTESY MINNESOTA HISTORICAL SOCIETY

BOTTOM RIGHT: *Great Northern Railway brochure.*
COURTESY JOHN CHASE COLLECTION AND
BURLINGTON-NORTHERN-SANTA FE RAILWAY

Through Your Car Window
EASTBOUND
On the Streamlined
EMPIRE BUILDER
and other Great Northern Trains

RIGHT: *Land postcard.*
COURTESY JOHN CHASE COLLECTION
AND BURLINGTON-NORTHERN-
SANTA FE RAILWAY

BELOW: *Great Northern*
work train crossing the plains.
PHOTOGRAPHER UNKNOWN. GNRR F3/7,
COURTESY MONTANA HISTORICAL SOCIETY

CHAPTER 3

CHANGING THE DIRECTION OF THE WEST

Although it slowed work on the St. Paul, Minneapolis & Manitoba main line, Hill's plan for building a financially sound railroad without government subsidy was to create revenue as he laid track. He had to fill the land with people and farms, and construct branch lines to bring their cattle, grain, timber, and ore to his railroad as he went. He did not have land grants to sell off, but there were vast acres of land in Dakota and Montana available for individual homesteaders under the 1862 Homestead Act. Just as Hill had vigorously promoted settlement of the Red River Valley, he would bring cattlemen, sheepmen, and farmers to Dakota and Montana. *Go West, Young Man*—to Hill—was northwest.

He had been a farmer in his youth and was particularly interested in wheat farming. He imagined an endless sea of golden wheat gently waving in the winds on the High Plains. He also knew that wheat fields along his line west would bring revenue to his railroad. He recruited immigrants in the East and in Europe, and populated a million acres with wheat farmers. He created an agronomy department for the railroad, hiring various experts to advise on methods for successfully farming the plains. His experts recommended deep plowing, crop rotation, and leaving fields fallow in alternating seasons.

It worked until a dry cycle came during the mid-1880s and produced one of the first great dustbowls in the American West. Hill had created a farming disaster. A common ditty at the time was "Twixt Hill and Hell, there's just one letter, if Hill were in Hell I'd feel much better." Hill put his then-enlightened agronomy department busy finding ways to help the farmers. The farmers learned new techniques, and every year Hill gave them three boxcar-loads of high-quality seed grains. The farmers recovered and increased the wheat yield by a third.

Hill was also a stockman. He imported Polled Angus from Scotland, increased his personal herd, and gave away 7,000 head of purebred breeding stock to improve

Pile-driving on the Missouri River in Montana Territory, 1887.
PHOTOGRAPHER UNKNOWN. GNRR F2/7, COURTESY MONTANA HISTORICAL SOCIETY

the stock roaming Dakota and Montana cattle ranches.

As tracks were slowly being laid westward, Hill either built or persuaded others to build stockyards and grain elevators for loading grain and cattle. By the end of 1884, St. Paul, Minneapolis & Manitoba tracks crossed 1,307 miles in Minnesota and Dakota Territory.

The land between Minot and the Rocky Mountains was mostly Indian reservations, which presented a problem to Hill's westward movement. For railroads to enter or cross reservations required *express permission from Congress.* This federal law had been circumvented by the other railroads, largely because the government was interested in their success. Hill was building without government interest or subsidy. He chose not to take a chance on "harassment by the government" and introduced a bill to change the law. It didn't pass. Hill discovered that Jay Gould of the Union Pacific had influenced its defeat. He barged into Gould's office in blazing-eyed fury, threatening to tear down the whole business and nail their ears to the capitol doors. Hill was too capable and too powerful to ignore. Another bill with the same provisions was introduced and passed.

In 1886 Hill was ready to lay track to the Great Falls of the Missouri in Montana Territory. Now, he was in a hurry! The other railroads were eyeing the rich resources of the northwest, which Hill considered his domain. The Union Pacific already had a subsidiary line from Ogden to Butte. Hill *poured the coal* to his plan to capture the Northwest's railroad business, particularly the lucrative freight shipments of the Butte copper mines. At the same time, Great Falls was emerging as an industrial town under the push and persistence of Hill's longtime friend Paris Gibson. Gibson had acquired title to power sites at the Missouri River waterfalls and purchased nearby coal sites, and was embarked on a plan to bring new industry to the city on the falls. At Hill's urging Gibson and other of Hill's friends organized the Montana Central Railroad Company. While the Montana Central began laying track south from Great

ABOVE: *Laying track of the St. Paul, Minneapolis & Manitoba, predecessor of the Great Northern Railway, from Minot, Dakota Territory, to Helena, Montana Territory. Construction began west of Minot April 2, 1887, and the rails reached Helena November 19, 1887.*
PHOTOGRAPHER UNKNOWN. GNRR F3/7,
COURTESY MONTANA HISTORICAL SOCIETY

BELOW: *Track-laying crew pose for photograph commemorating their August 11, 1887 track laying record of eight miles in one day. Note the Fort Assinniboine band on hand for the celebration. September 8, 1887.*
PHOTOGRAPHER UNKNOWN. GNRR F3/7,
COURTESY MONTANA HISTORICAL SOCIETY

COMMISSIONERS to the World's Fair from twenty foreign countries, and speaking sixteen different languages, took a look at the farming districts of Minnesota and North Dakota in the autumn of 1893, as guests of the Great Northern Railway. They expressed surprise at the agricultural thrift and prosperity, and wondered at the large proportion of educated and cultivated people they met in the villages and on the farms, comparing most favorably with country life in European countries. The secret of this is that the Northwest is largely composed of transplanted communities, the railways having taken people there by the wholesale. The Northwest knows nothing of the frontier life that lasted for a generation in the valley of Mississippi before the era of railways. Towns and cities spring up like magic in the new West. Grain elevators seem to stand everywhere along the horizon, like ships at sea. This view was taken at Larimore, N. D., where the commissioners saw sixty-five self-binders cutting wheat in a single field.

30

ABOVE: *World's Fair Commissioners on the Larimore Farm in North Dakota.*
VALLEY, PLAIN & PEAK: SCENES ALONG THE LINE OF THE GREAT NORTHERN, GREAT NORTHERN 1894 BOOKLET; COURTESY K. ROSS TOOLE ARCHIVES, UNIVERSITY OF MONTANA, MISSOULA

BELOW: *Irrigation scene near Great Falls, Montana.*
VALLEY, PLAIN & PEAK: SCENES ALONG THE LINE OF THE GREAT NORTHERN, GREAT NORTHERN 1894 BOOKLET; COURTESY K. ROSS TOOLE ARCHIVES, UNIVERSITY OF MONTANA, MISSOULA

THE question of artificially supplying moisture to crops in the western half of the United States is becoming an important one. Water for this purpose is abundant in Montana and Washington in the rivers and lakes, and storage basins are easily made. In the Dakotas the largest and strongest artesian basin in the world is being utilized for both irrigation and power. The wells of Dakota are often of such force and volume as to supply towns with water for fire purposes. Irrigation is no new problem, for half of the people of the earth live on foods raised by this method. The farmer of irrigated districts does not wait for rain when his crops are dry; he uses water at will.

"Mighty as has been our past our resources have just been touched upon, and there is wealth beyond the Mississippi which, in the not distant future, will astonish even the dwellers by Lake Michigan. * * My waking dreams have been filled with visions of the incalculable wealth which the touch of water will bring to life from those great uncultivated plains toward the Pacific. The same power which wastes millions on the Mississippi can be utilized to make the desert bloom with the homes of men, and bring forth the fruits of the Garden of Eden."—*Thos. B. Reed, at Pittsburg,* **April, 1894.**

44

GREAT FALLS has its name from the great falls of the Missouri River, first made known through the explorations of Lewis and Clarke. The city has many important industries scattered along a water-power sufficient to turn the wheels of a nation's machinery, and generates enough electricity for a continent's use. The river has a width of 2,800 feet opposite the city front, but narrows to 1,000 feet a half-mile below, preparatory to the first leap in the series of falls, the aggregate plunge amounting to 520 feet. Close to the first, or Black Eagle Falls, a giant spring bursts from the bank twenty feet above the river, in volume sufficient to make a stream 200 feet wide and five feet deep. Rainbow Falls, the prettiest of the number, has a drop of full fifty feet, and ranks next to the Great Falls, where the mighty stream leaps ninety feet. Unlike the turbid river it becomes in the prairie States, the water here is clear. From one point of observation three different falls, the giant spring, and five ranges of mountains can be seen.

"It is altogether a wild and splendid spectacle."—*Charles Dudley Warner in Harper's Magazine.*

40

ABOVE: *Copper Smelter and Refinery, Great Falls, Montana.*
VALLEY, PLAIN & PEAK: SCENES ALONG THE LINE OF THE GREAT NORTHERN, GREAT NORTHERN 1894 BOOKLET; K. ROSS TOOLE ARCHIVES, UNIVERSITY OF MONTANA

BELOW: *Hotel Broadwater and Natatorium, Helena Hot Springs, Montana.*
VALLEY, PLAIN & PEAK: SCENES ALONG THE LINE OF THE GREAT NORTHERN, GREAT NORTHERN 1894 BOOKLET; K. ROSS TOOLE ARCHIVES, UNIVERSITY OF MONTANA

IF THERE is a city in the world built literally on a gold mine it is Helena; the precious dust is still gathered from the very streets and washed from the sands of neighboring streams and rivulets. The heaps of stones and gravel in sight on all sides attest that search for the yellow dross still continues. From its principal street, the old-time "Last Chance" gulch, gold equal to the fortunes of millionaires has been taken. Helena has long been an important center, and is one of the richest cities per capita in the country. A notable feature is the Hot Springs, with Hotel Broadwater and its wonderful Natatorium. The latter is the finest specimen of Moorish architecture in America; its vaulted roof of cathedral glass covers a bathing pool 300 by 100 feet in size, with enormous water supply.

"That portion of the Great Northwest, starting from the west slope of the Cascade Range, running east to Helena, Montana, and north from the Columbia and Snake rivers into British Columbia, contains more wealth in gold, silver, copper, iron, lead, coal, etc., than any other part of the earth."—*Ex-U. S. Senator Warner Miller, in a speech on the Nicaragua Canal.*

48

BUTTE is a mining city, one of the most important in the world. It produces millions of pounds of copper every year, and silver and gold equal to the revenue of a principality. The ground under the city is honeycombed with tunnels and drifts, and palatial business blocks, pretty homes, and mining industries are mixed up in veritable confusion. Even if generations of constant working should exhaust the endowment of precious metals, Montana will still have coal and iron, a fine grazing country, vast tracts of well timbered land and wide stretches of fertile valleys and plains; and these resources are made available by the railways built under the stimulus of the mines. Butte is picturesque, and the railways getting in and out are very much tangled up in the mountains. The first view of the city, after the Great Northern train from Helena and the East emerges from among the rocks, is one of the most striking in the country.

50

Falls to the territorial capital in Helena and the mines in Butte, Hill was pushing the St. Paul, Minneapolis & Manitoba Railroad line west from Minot across the plains of Montana to connect to the Montana Central at Great Falls.

The slow, deliberate pace that had marked construction across Dakota to Minot now shifted into a furious back-breaking, man-killing pace. In March 1887 Hill's men worked day and night setting up camp and bringing men and materials to the railhead at Minot. By the first of April, 8,000 men and 3,300 teams were grading roadbed, and 650 men and 225 teams were laying track and building bridges. In seven and half months, 643 miles of main and feeder track were laid, averaging three and half miles per day. A record eight miles were laid between daylight and dark on August 11, 1887.

By 1888, the fifty-year-old Hill had extended his lines in the west to Great Falls, connecting to Helena and Butte, but his ambition to push on to the Pacific had not wavered. On

September 16, 1889, he organized the Great Northern Railway Company. The Great Northern leased the property of the St. Paul, Minneapolis & Manitoba for 999 years and at midnight on January 31, 1890, the Great Northern took over 2,770 miles of track. At the next board meeting the directors decided to extend the lines west to the coast.

ABOVE: *The mining city of Butte, Montana.*

VALLEY, PLAIN & PEAK: SCENES ALONG THE LINE OF THE GREAT NORTHERN, GREAT NORTHERN 1894 BOOKLET; COURTESY K. ROSS TOOLE ARCHIVES, UNIVERSITY OF MONTANA, MISSOULA

BELOW: *Interior of the Broadwater Natatorium, Helena, Montana.*

COURTESY COLLECTION OF ROBERT SMITH

Marias, the Pass that Wouldn't Stay Found

Without the luxury of government assistance, Hill had to build the Great Northern better than the subsidized transcontinental lines. He told his engineers that they should never tackle a grade that could be avoided. They managed to get through 400 miles of Montana with no grade exceeding 31.7 feet to the mile. Then they came up against the high, rugged Rocky Mountains. Hill had heard of a pass that the Indians used in ancient times and that explorers had long tried to find. When he started to build his lines west he had already decided that he would find the lost pass for his railroad.

The story of Marias Pass is one of Blackfeet legend, explorer's lore, and chance discovery. Although men of the Lewis and Clark Expedition had walked nearby, this lowest and easiest pass across the Rocky Mountains lay shrouded in mist and fog, hidden from them. It would remain unexplored by whites long after more tortuous passes across the Rockies had been trudged by trappers, mapped by explorers, and traversed by gold seekers and settlers. Had this easily traversed northwest passage across the Rockies been discovered by Lewis and Clark it would undoubtedly have changed the path of settlement of the west.

The destiny of this hidden pass is rooted in the legendary fierce reputation of the Blackfeet Indians. These Indians are believed to be an Algonquian nation who had moved westward from the Slave Lakes in northern Canada. They acquired guns and ammunition from French and British traders and raided the southern tribes to get Spanish horses in the 1700s. They were strategically skilled warriors, driving the other tribes off the buffalo ranges of the plains and across the mountains, claiming future central Montana as their own and defending it against invaders. Tales of the terrible Blackfeet were passed on by Kutenai, Flathead, Cheyenne, and Shoshone Indians, mountain men, and fur traders.

When Lewis and Clark made their journey west in 1804 to 1806 to explore the country acquired by the Louisiana Purchase they had only one serious encounter with hostile Indians. After crossing the Bitterroot Mountains on their homeward journey, the expedition divided into two parties. They took different routes and were to meet at the mouth of the Yellowstone. Lewis headed north to the Great Falls of the Missouri, and then to seek the headwaters of the Marias River. They had first seen this fork of the Missouri River on their westward trek to the Columbia and named it Maria's River for Lewis' cousin Maria Wood or, as some historians claim,

BOTTOM: *Marias River.*
COURTESY K. ROSS TOOLE ARCHIVES, UNIVERSITY OF MONTANA, MISSOULA AND BURLINGTON-NORTHERN-SANTA FE RAILWAY

BELOW: *Blackfeet Indians Near the Rockies.*
COURTESY K. ROSS TOOLE ARCHIVES, UNIVERSITY OF MONTANA, MISSOULA AND BURLINGTON-NORTHERN-SANTA FE RAILWAY

for one of Lewis' many romantic attachments. Lewis' mission was to discover the latitude at the river's source, which could extend the northern boundary of the Louisiana Purchase (defined as all land drained by the Missouri River system).

Lewis and three other men camped on what would become known as Cut Bank Creek then started back toward the Missouri. On the bluffs overlooking the Two Medicine Lodges River, they came upon eight Indians driving a herd of horses. They believed the Indians were the dreaded Blackfeet. Lewis and Clark had heard from several tribes they encountered that the Blackfeet terrorized other tribes and were the most feared warriors on the plains.

Lewis greeted the Indians cautiously and gave the leaders a medal, a flag, and a handkerchief. They all rode down the bluff to the river and camped that night below the mouth of Badger Creek. The next morning the Americans woke to discover an Indian taking their guns. Two of Lewis' men grabbed the Indian and, while struggling to get the gun, stabbed the warrior in the heart. Meanwhile Lewis chased two of the Indians into a gulch. One turned and fired and Lewis shot him. The other Indians mounted their ponies and rode away. Lewis and his men rounded up four of their six horses and nine of the Indian ponies and hurriedly left the encampment before the Indians could return with more warriors. In John C. Jackson's book *The Piikani Blackfeet: a Culture under Siege*, he suggests that the Blackfeet reaction to the incident was not as bad as Lewis and the fleeing Americans feared. It was a war game. But the encounter added to the store of tales of the terrible Blackfeet and altered the path of American exploration and development.

TOP: *Blackfeet Indians on the trail.*
COURTESY GLACIER NATIONAL PARK ARCHIVES

CENTER: *The old travois trail, Glacier National Park.*
COURTESY GLACIER NATIONAL PARK ARCHIVES

BOTTOM: *Blackfeet Indian council.*
COURTESY COLLECTION OF ROBERT SMITH

Blackfeet Indians on the Trail.

THE OLD TRAVOIS TRAIL, GLACIER NATIONAL PARK, MONTANA
Courtesy R. W. Reed Kalispell

5835. Blackfeet Indian Council, Lake McDermott Region, Glacier National Park, Montana. See America First

Shrouded in mist, cloaked in mystery, and guarded by fear of the Blackfeet, the peerless Marias Pass across the mountains was known to exist, but remained unexplored for another eighty-four years while wagon trains of immigrants headed west over the more arduous Oregon and California trails.

Shortly following Lewis' visit, David Thompson, a partner in the Northwest Fur Company who explored and mapped the territory from Hudson Bay to the Pacific Ocean, reported in his journals that in 1810 about 150 Flatheads and the white traders Finan McDonald, Michael Bourdeaux, and Baptiste Buch crossed the mountains by a "wide defile of easy passage eastward of Selish [Flathead] Lake" to hunt buffalo. They were ambushed by the Blackfeet, but had been warned and managed to defeat their attackers. The Blackfeet blamed their defeat on the white trappers who had armed their Flathead enemies with guns, although they had obtained theirs the same way.

The angry Blackfeet made it known that any white man found in Blackfeet territory would be considered an enemy. In 1812, the Flathead and two white trappers used Cut Bank Pass farther north to cross to the buffalo, but they were attacked by the ever watchful Blackfeet and forced to withdraw and do their hunting elsewhere. The Blackfeet became even more vigilant in guarding the passes across their part of the Rockies. Trappers avoided the area; instead Indians took the furs from the Marias region to the trading posts at Fort Piegan and Fort Benton.

Scholar and historian Robert Greenhow mapped the region for the fur companies in 1840. Although there is no record of his actually having been there, he marked Marias Pass as the "Route across the Mts" on his map published as part of his *Memoir Historical and Political of the North West Coast of North America*. Many early maps were compiled from actual exploration and many were drawn from the accounts of trappers and Indians. Greenhow's map was amazingly accurate, with the pass's location probably provided by Indians or trappers. The passage across the Rockies would continue to escape recorded discovery for another fifteen years.

In March 1853, Congress allotted $150,000 to Secretary of War Jefferson Davis to survey four possible routes for a transcontinental railroad to the Pacific. The surveys were to be completed in ten months. Isaac I. Stevens, once a major in the United States Army Engineering Corps and then the zealous governor of the newly created Washington Territory, which included future Montana, led the survey of the northern route from the Great Lakes to Puget Sound between the 49th and the 47th parallels. Railroads required grades no steeper than 116 feet to the mile and curves with a minimum 300-foot radius to keep a locomotive from jumping the track. A suitable pass through the Rockies was critical to Stevens' desired northern transcontinental railroad route.

Fear of the Blackfeet still influenced exploration in the north. Although Stevens reported that Chief Little Dog of the Piegan tribe of the Blackfeet described Marias Pass to him and that his contact with the Blackfeet was "uniformly friendly and our intercourse with the several tribes of the Blackfeet nation was especially of the most cordial character," the Flathead guide and other members of Stevens' survey party refused to go any farther into Blackfeet territory. This was true of other guides and explorers, some insisting that a small army of men accompany them through the territory or refusing altogether. Stevens sent engineer A.W. Tinkham to find the pass.

Tinkham and a Flathead scout started on the western side of the Rockies, traveling north through the Flathead Valley then eastward. They

Back cover of Great Northern Railway trail riding brochure.
COURTESY K. ROSS TOOLE ARCHIVES, UNIVERSITY OF MONTANA, MISSOULA

followed an old Indian trail up Nyack Creek and crossed at Cut Bank Pass in what is now Glacier National Park. They crossed the Continental Divide at 7,600 feet. It was October and frigid—3 degrees above zero. Tinkham, cold, believing that he had crossed the long-sought Marias Pass, fearing the Blackfeet and prompted by his Flathead scout, hurried on to Fort Benton to make his report to Stevens. Tinkham stated that he had found the pass and described the country as "narrow, wooded and precipitous, with a bare rocky ridge offering foothold for a horse, but by no means practicable for the passage of wagons." Some historians believe that Tinkham's hurry to get through Blackfeet territory caused him to miss Marias Pass altogether. However, terrain approaching the pass from the west is more deceptive than that from the east and may, in part, account for Tinkham's misreckoning.

Stevens was not satisfied with Tinkham's report. He believed Chief Little Dog's description of Marias Pass and, to him, find-

FORT ASSINNIBOINE is the largest military post in the United States. The quarters are of brick, and the cost of construction to 1894 amounts to more than $2,000,000. A full regiment of troops is usually stationed there. The location is sightly, on a clear stream in the foothills of the Bear Paw Mountains. It is in full view from the Great Northern car windows.

Two Medicine is a pretty lake nestling in the eastern slope of the Rockies, near Midvale Station. The story of the name is that many years ago the Blackfoot tribe had a civil war and the two factions agreed to a council on the shores of the lake, each party erecting its own medicine lodge. Peace was agreed upon, and the name attaches to the lake and to the two streams leading away from it to Marias River, so named by Lewis and Clarke, in honor of Maria, the wife of a member of their party.

36

ing it was imperative to a northern route for the first transcontinental railroad. He was determined to find a way to lead the railroad through his domain of Washington Territory. However, the funds he was allotted for the survey were nearly used up. He wrote to Jefferson Davis of his intent to continue the survey and that he believed the Congress would agree and fund the additional costs. In the spring of 1854 he sent engineer James Doty to look for the pass from the eastern side. Doty's scout was Hugh Monroe, known by the Blackfeet as Rising Wolf. Monroe came to work for the Hudson's Bay Company in 1815 as a trapper and interpreter. He was then sixteen years old, and by the time he was twenty-four, he had quit Hudson's Bay, adopted the ways of the Blackfeet, married an Indian girl, and begun to live among the Indians (as he would for over thirty years).

Doty and Monroe explored the Rockies' front range, passed the trail that Tinkham claimed was Marias Pass, went north toward what is now known as Lower St. Mary Lake, then southward to explore an old Indian trail—Doty all the while listening to Monroe's stories of the fierce Blackfeet. They entered the mountains through a gap fifteen miles wide. Doty believed he had discovered the east entrance and sent word to Stevens. Doty's jubilance over possibly finding the pass was short-lived. Jefferson Davis, who favored a southern railroad route, sent Stevens a scathing message to stop any further search for the mysterious pass. Reluctantly, Stevens sent word to Doty to return to Fort Benton without delay. He never explored the pass to make sure. The northern trail was abandoned as a possible route for the nation's first transcontinental railroad. The elusive Marias Pass was *lost* for another thirty-five years.

James Hill's railroad had reached Havre, Montana, turned southwest to Great Falls, Helena, Butte, and White Sulphur Springs by 1889, but Hill also wanted a railroad straight west from Havre. He was determined to take his railroad the most direct route west to the Pacific and over the lowest possible grades. He had brought his railroad through 400 miles of Montana with no grade exceeding

St. Paul, Minneapolis & Manitoba, later Great Northern, office car. Fort Assinniboine, Montana, 1887.

PHOTOGRAPHER UNKNOWN. GNRR F3/7, COURTESY MONTANA HISTORICAL SOCIETY

31.7 feet to the mile. To take the line over the Rockies at the lowest possible grade meant finding Marias Pass.

Hill hired John F. Stevens, and charged him with finding the pass. The thirty-six-year-old Stevens started in his profession as an axman and rodman in surveying parties and worked his way through increasing levels of responsibility to become a respected location engineer. He helped lay routes for the Milwaukee, the Duluth, and the Canadian Pacific and earned an enviable reputation in planning the route of the Denver & Rio Grande narrow-gauge railroad. He was known as one of the best mountain-country location engineers in the nation.

Stevens set out from Fort Assinniboine traveling west. He had a wagon, a mule, and a saddle horse. A hundred and sixty miles westward, he came to the Blackfeet Agency on Badger Creek and tried to hire a Blackfeet to serve as guide. But no Blackfeet would accompany him. Historians differ on the reason the Blackfeet would not take Stevens into the pass. When Stevens arrived, the proud, nomadic Blackfeet had been ravaged by smallpox, traders' whiskey, the Indian and white man wars of the 1860s and 1870s, the near extinction of the buffalo herds, and the starvation winter of 1883. They were living on the Blackfeet Reservation, which included all of what is now Glacier National Park. They were no longer fiercely guarding vast territorial hunting grounds. Some believe that the continuing Blackfeet taboo about the pass was their belief that it was a haunt of evil spirits. The Blackfeet taboo may have been more strategic than spiritual. These proud people of the plains were already the victims of the white man's invasion into their territorial hunting grounds. They must have known that another railroad would bring more settlers and crowd them into an ever shrinking reservation. There was no reason or will to aid the discovery of Marias Pass.

John Stevens was able to convince Coonsah, a Flathead guide, to go along. When Stevens and Coonsah headed out it was December and the snow too deep for the horses to get through. They strung rawhide into snow shoes and began their journey across a brutally cold, white expanse. Several miles east of the pass, Coonsah stated he would go no farther. Stevens decided to go on alone. He had studied Greenhow's 1840 map, Isaac Stevens' and Tinkham's and Doty's reports, and the Blackfeet description of the pass. By chance or reckoning he walked right into it. Then he continued on, crossing the Continental Divide and dropping into the western drainage.

Certain that he had crossed the Divide and

Stevens Monument at Marias Pass.
KERRY T. NICKOU PHOTO

satisfied that he had found the lost pass across the Rockies, he turned back and camped at the summit. It was bitter cold. The temperature was forty below zero and falling. Stevens didn't dare lie down for fear of lapsing into the dreamy sleep of freezing cold from which he would never awake. He built a fire and tramped back and forth all night. At daybreak he set out for the agency at Badger Creek. He came across the nearly frozen Coonsah, whose fire had gone out during the night. Stevens revived him and the two went on to the agency to make their report. He had found the Marias Pass.

Stevens reported to Hill that the approach to the pass was broad and open, the pass is a low open valley from one to six miles wide, the summit only 5,200 feet high, and could be reached by a grade of less than 100 feet to the mile. Little excavation of solid rock work would be necessary. He estimated the cost of the road through the pass would not exceed $16,000 per mile; as the route to the coast, it would be at least 100 miles shorter than any other.

On August 1, 1890, the Great Northern awarded railroad contractor Shepard, Seims & Company a contract to construct 188 miles of road from Fort Assinniboine to the base of the mountains near the entrance to Marias Pass. The route became known as the Assiniboine Route. A subsequent contract would be awarded for the work through the pass and down the western slope. The work was to begin immediately and be completed in five months. Within a fortnight Shepard, Seims & Company sent eight hundred teams and two thousand men to begin work.

Stevens would continue as principal engineer of the Great Northern Railway, taking the line west following the Flathead River, the Kootenai and the Clark Fork and through the cascades to Puget Sound. He would go on to become operating chief of the Chicago, Rock Island & Pacific Railroad, and in 1905 chief engineer of the Panama Canal. He took over operation

and construction for the New York, New Haven & Hartford in New England, and the Spokane, Portland & Seattle on the Pacific Coast. He went to Russia as head of the American Railway Advisory Commission to reorganize the Trans-Siberian and Chinese railways and keep open the line between Vladivostok and Moscow. In March 1925 he received the American Engineers highest honor—the John Fritz medal.

Magazine advertisement.
COURTESY JOHN CHASE COLLECTION AND BURLINGTON-NORTHERN-SANTA FE RAILWAY

Rolling through the Rockies

YOUR uniformed sons and daughters, traveling over America on the Great Northern Railway, cross the Continental Divide almost without knowing it. The train follows a natural route—easy as a game trail—through the scenic grandeur of the Montana Rockies. That is Marias Pass!

At the top of the pass—at Summit, Montana—they see a statue of its discoverer, John F. Stevens, who still is living. In December, 1889, Stevens found a broad, natural corridor through the Rockies, which provided the lowest (5,213 feet) and easiest railway pass in the northern United States.

Stevens' discovery not only gave Great Northern its low-altitude pass through the mountains, it also led to establishment of Glacier National Park—the only national park on the main line of an American railway.

Manpower, firepower and supplies for America and her Allies are rolling through the Rockies faster and on time because Marias Pass affords swifter, safer handling of trains.

Marias Pass helps make Great Northern dependable—a vital artery to Victory.

GREAT NORTHERN RAILWAY

ROUTE OF THE EMPIRE BUILDER BETWEEN THE GREAT LAKES AND THE PACIFIC

RIGHT: *Sunset on Mt. Rockwell, Glacier National Park.*
COURTESY GLACIER NATIONAL PARK ARCHIVES

BELOW: *These rolling triple-decker bunkhouses were home to the workmen and train crews of the St. Paul, Minneapolis & Manitoba, later the Great Northern, while extending the line west from Minot, Dakota Territory, to the Pacific. These cars had to be sawn down to clear the tunnels.*
GREAT NORTHERN PHOTOGRAPH.
COURTESY MINNESOTA HISTORICAL SOCIETY

"(c) Kiser Photo Co., Portland, Oregon."

SUNSET ON MT. ROCKWELL, GLACIER NATIONAL PARK, MONTANA

CHAPTER 4

Hear that Train a-Comin'

When the surveyors and engineers finished their jobs, the dangerous backbreaking task of actually building the line began. The men who worked on the railroad came from all over; some were veterans of other railroads, but most were immigrants desperate for work. Irish, Germans, Scots, Swedes, Norwegians, Italians, and Greeks labored to lay track.

Roustabouts—rugged, hardened men with shovels and dumpcarts—cleared paths while sweat-lathered horses and mules strained against their harnesses pulling massive trees aside, clearing boulders from the path, and dragging scrapers across the resistant rocky land that would form the road bed. When the roadbed was ready, horse-drawn wagons piled high with ties moved along it while crews tossed ties off the wagon and into place. Then the track-layers came.

The rails were brought to within a half mile of the railhead on flatcars, loaded onto a horse-drawn car, and galloped to a pile of spikes, bolts, and rail couplings stacked for the day's work. These supplies were quickly loaded onto the cart and galloped to the front of the last pair of rails that had been spiked down. Two men hurriedly pulled the rails off in pairs and started forward while the rest of the five-man-per-rail gang took hold by twos until the 500-pound rail was clear

of the car. They went forward at a run, and on command from the gang boss they dropped the rail in place. As soon as the rails were down, men with notched wooden gauges stepped in and spaced each pair of rails four feet, eight and one half inches apart. Then the spike men swung their mauls—thirty spikes to the rail, three blows to the spike. The empty cart was pulled to the side to make way for the next car running up then sent back for another stack of rails, spikes, bolts, and couplings.

The work train followed the newly laid track. It was a rolling town, a center of operations. A locomotive pushed the work train along the newly laid track to within half a mile of the railhead, or end of track. Leading the work train were flatcars carrying the tools and the blacksmith shop. Next were triple-decker bunkhouses that were home

Track-laying crew poses for photograph, Montana Territory, 1887.
PHOTOGRAPHER UNKNOWN. GNRR F3/7, #43327-B, COURTESY MONTANA HISTORICAL SOCIETY

U.S. Standard Railroad Gauge

The U.S. standard for distance between rails is 4 feet, 8.5 inches, roughly the width of two horse rumps. There's a good reason for this unusual standard.

Imperial Rome built the first long-distance roads in Europe and England for their legions to conquer the world. The Roman war chariots formed wheel ruts. Later builders of wagons and carts spaced their wheels to match the chariot wheel ruts rather than risk destroying their wagon wheels on the deeply rutted roads that laced the countryside. In the 1500s, Germany began to use wagonways made of wooden rails laid over dirt roads. By that time the wheel width of two horse rumps wide was becoming the standard.

In the 1700s, iron rails replaced the wooden rails, and wheels on carts and the wagonways evolved into tramways. The tramways were built using the same wheel spacing that was used for building the early wagonways, and then when the first rail lines were built they used the same jigs and tools and spacing used to build the tramways. The chariots, the wagons, the wagonways, and the tramways were all powered by horses. When the U.S. imported its first locomotives, they were designed to run on the tramways of Europe. And when we built the first U.S. railroads they matched the wheel spacing of the tramways. Two Roman-war-horse-rumps wide became the U.S. standard.

ABOVE: *Workers gather in front of the dining car for the photographer. A group of friendly Indian visitors stand in the front. Montana Territory 1887.*
GREAT NORTHERN PHOTOGRAPH. COURTESY MINNESOTA HISTORICAL SOCIETY

RIGHT: *Steam shovel cutting path on the mountainsides of Marias Pass. The Great Northern worktrain waits steaming in the background.*
GREAT NORTHERN PHOTOGRAPH. COURTESY COLLECTION OF JOHN CHASE, GREAT FALLS, MT

BELOW: *Original Two-Medicine Bridge crosses the river east of Marias Pass.*
GREAT NORTHERN PHOTOGRAPH.
COURTESY STUMPTOWN
HISTORICAL SOCIETY,
WHITEFISH, MT

for the men grading the roadbed, laying track, and operating the train. Hill's triple-deckers were designed to house as many men as possible on a single flatcar, but often, there were more men than bunks and some needed to sleep outside on top. The triple-deckers had to be sawn down to get through the tunnels in the mountains.

Next to the bunkhouse was the dining car, with a single table running its full length. It was laden with buckets of coffee, great plates of bread, and platters of meat, potatoes, and beans. The men ate in shifts. "Eat fast and get out" was the rule. They rushed in, gulped down huge plates of food and left. The kitchen and store-room cars followed behind the dining car. Often the contractor-supplied meat, usually antelope, deer, or moose from the nearby woods, and sometimes beef, hung on hooks outside the car.

Far out in front of the track layers, bridge monkeys were building trestles over the Cutbank and Two-Medicine rivers with timber cut in the nearby woods. These hand-hewn

wooden trestles were built on the same general plan with a span or truss at the highest point and the joints hewed to a perfect fit. The Cutbank trestle was longer, but the most famous of the hand-hewn wooden trestles was the Two-Medicine Bridge—which is higher, standing 215 feet above a canyon. It took three-quarters of a million board feet of timber and forty-five days to complete. When it was in use and high winds came down the

Snowshed on Marias Pass.
COURTESY STUMPTOWN
HISTORICAL SOCIETY,
WHITEFISH, MT

Work crews building the snowsheds through Marias Pass along the southern border of Glacier National Park.
COURTESY STUMPTOWN
HISTORICAL SOCIETY,
WHITEFISH, MT

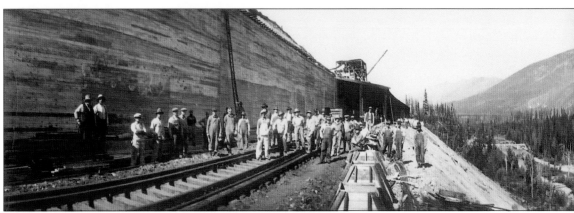

A Great Northern train steams past a snowshed under construction.
COURTESY STUMPTOWN
HISTORICAL SOCIETY,
WHITEFISH, MT

draw, the bridge would drift six feet out of line and back again while the engine waited impatiently to cross. These wooden bridges limited the size of the locomotives used on the line for many years. Both have since been replaced by steel bridges.

In the winter, the Rocky Mountains accumulate heavy layers of snow, with drifts in the passes as much as fifty to seventy-five feet deep. Once the railroads had figured out where to put the tracks across the rugged mountains, they had to find ways to deal with the winter snow while they were building track, and later when the trains were running. Keeping the line open and pushing the trains through the snow-covered passes is the stuff of railroad lore. Many a true tale is told of trains pushing their way through blizzards and merciless white drifts, a miserable few feet at a time, with only the shear power of a full-throttle locomotive and the cowcatcher to ram the heavy wall of snow.

The Great Northern tracks from East Glacier through Marias Pass run southwesterly along the southern slopes of Skelton Mountain, Blacktail Hills, Elk Mountain, Mount Shields, and Running Rabbit Mountain and then bend northerly around Running Rabbit on their path along the Middle Fork of the Flathead River to the Belton Station at West Glacier. Deep winter snows pile up and sudden slides are a spring ritual. The Great Northern railroad crews built a string of snowsheds along the most slide-prone slopes to protect the trains. Timber from the nearby forests was used for bracing, bents, purlins, sills, roof timbers, and cribbing. The roofs slant out and downward from the mountainside to deflect the snow and keep it from piling up. Toward spring, when the snows begin to melt, the vibration of an oncoming train often triggers a sudden avalanche. Many a train has reached the shelter of the snow shed just in time to be saved from being tumbled down the mountain by a wall of snow.

Great Northern snow crew at Summit, Montana, circa 1920. Keeping the main line through Marias Pass open in the winter was a constant battle against blizzards, snowslides, and blowing snow. A large work force was required to keep switches and sidings open.
PHOTOGRAPH BY J. R. BUHMILLER. COURTESY COLLECTION OF JOHN CHASE, GREAT FALLS, MT

A snow dozer on a cold March day in 1921 at Summit, Montana. The engineer was L. McCauley. Although the locomotive number is not clear enough to be read, John Chase, a railroad enthusiast since his youth, believes it is a class F-8, 2-8-0.
PHOTOGRAPH BY J. R. BUHMILLER. COURTESY COLLECTION OF JOHN CHASE, GREAT FALLS, MT

Great Northern officials drive the ceremonial last spike to complete the road on January 6, 1893, in the Cascade Mountains.
GREAT NORTHERN PHOTOGRAPH. COURTESY MINNESOTA HISTORICAL SOCIETY

Snow crews were assigned along the route in winter and worked night and day to shovel snow off the tracks, but when a blizzard hit or a storm dumped tons of snow all at once, a locomotive with rotary plow coupled to the engine, or a steel or steel-reinforced wooden plow mounted on the front end, was used to clear the tracks ahead of a train. Plowing or "bucking" snow was slow, hard, dangerous work. If the snow was dry and light, the snowdozer could easily clear a path, but if it was deep and heavily compacted the snowdozer might have to take several runs at it, backing up and charging the white mass at full throttle. If they were lucky the engine broke through and the train behind did not derail, but often the dozer and the train were stuck fast.

Hill built the nation's best transcontinental railroad economically by using superior engineering and paying low wages. Like the other builders of his time, he reasoned that the future advantages his railroad would bring to the country and the people vastly

Magazine ad.

COURTESY JOHN CHASE COLLECTION AND BURLINGTON-NORTHERN-SANTA FE RAILWAY

There are plenty more like this in
Glacier National Park

Come out this summer and try your black gnat in Lake Josephine or other snow-fed lakes and streams in the Park. Go camera-hunting for Rocky Mountain goats and bighorn sheep. Hike or ride horseback through valleys of wild flowers, explore interesting glaciers. Modern hotels and chalets provide every comfort.

The New Oriental Limited takes you direct to the gate of Glacier National Park, which, with Waterton Lakes National Park just across the boundary in Canada, forms a vast international playground. Special low summer fares. Inquire today.

GREAT NORTHERN
ROUTE OF THE NEW ORIENTAL LIMITED

A dependable railway

Mail the Coupon

A. J. Dickinson, Passenger Traffic Manager
Great Northern Railway, St. Paul, Minn.

Send me free books describing recreation in Glacier National Park.
☐ General Tour of Parks
☐ Pacific Northwest Coast Tours
☐ Burlington Escorted Tours

Name

Address

outweighed the grumbling of the impoverished men who actually put track on the ground. His contract with the Sheppard, Seims & Company to build line westward from Havre was money tight. In January 1891, the corporation posted its wage scales: foremen $50 to $70 per week, cooks $35 to $60, teamsters $30, blacksmiths $40, laborers $2 per day. The men had to pay board of $5 per week. By September, they were coming off the line by the hundreds in protest over poor wages and poor food, and the foremen were predicting a work slowdown. But times were tough, and the tote road—the road where men-wanted-for-work signs were posted—stayed continuously lined with men. Minor compromises were made and the work went on. It would not be until 1894, well after the Great Northern line was completed to the coast, that the men working on branch lines staged an effective strike. The American Railroad Union declared it the most singular victory ever won by organized labor. Newspapers announced "J.J. Hill Sunstruck" and "Right against Might."

By the middle of December 1891, track had been laid through Marias Pass around the border of Glacier and as far west as Columbia Falls. In February 1892 it moved west of Kalispell headed toward track being laid east from Spokane. (Years later the main line to Kalispell would be abandoned in favor of the line to Whitefish.) Meanwhile John Stevens was locating the route from Spokane across the prairies and hills of central Washington along the Wenatchee River, then west through the Cascade Range and on to Everett where the line connected to the Seattle & Montana Railroad to the coast.

The last rail of the Great Northern's 834-mile track from Havre, Montana, to the Puget Sound was laid on January 6, 1893, at Scenic, Washington. The line from St. Paul to Seattle covered 1,816 miles and was 115 miles shorter than that of the Northern Pacific.

TUMWATER CANYON is the valley of the Wenatchee River narrowed to a chasm, which, in scenic grandeur, has no rival elsewhere possible to see from the car windows. The river is a series of cascades playing leap-frog over giant stones. Now for a moment it rests in an eddy or hisses in the shallows, and then leaps against resisting rocks and becomes white with foam, and roars above the noise of the train. Streams like white ribbons are flung down from the lofty snow-fields, it not being possible to tell where the stream begins or the snow ends. What looks like moss on the distant hills is a forest of pine trees. Walls of rock rise to dizzy heights, and the river alongside boils angrily. Every rod forward presents new scenes, from merely picturesque to exalted and sublime, and one constantly feels with each that no other can furnish so fair and grand a sight.

"As we passed through the Rockies we thought the scenery could not be surpassed, but as we descended into the valley of the Columbia and out of that valley into the Cascade Mountains, we found the scenery grander than that we just left."—*Interview in St. Paul Pioneer Press with Mgr. Satolli.*

76

ABOVE: *In Tumwater (Talking Water) Canyon, Washington.*
VALLEY, PLAIN & PEAK: SCENES ALONG THE LINE OF THE GREAT NORTHERN, GREAT NORTHERN 1894 BOOKLET; K. ROSS TOOLE ARCHIVES, UNIVERSITY OF MONTANA

BELOW: *On the "Switchback" in the Cascade Mountains, Washington.*
VALLEY, PLAIN & PEAK: SCENES ALONG THE LINE OF THE GREAT NORTHERN, GREAT NORTHERN 1894 BOOKLET; K. ROSS TOOLE ARCHIVES, UNIVERSITY OF MONTANA

THE "SWITCHBACK" is a term applied to the engineering contrivance which enables the trains of the Great Northern to switch back and forth in getting over the Cascade range, where mountains are terraced off in such numbers that they can not be counted, and peak, glacier, canyon, waterfall and snowdrift intermingled to the bewilderment of the beholder. Each stretch of track is called a leg. There are three legs on the east side and four on the west. The monster iron horses, hitched tandem, haul the cars with seeming ease across the mighty barrier. From one leg or ledge to another the splendid engines keep their steadfast course, for every precaution possible to model management is faithfully observed. The track, like the house of the wise man of the scriptures, is "builded on a rock," and the granite way is as safe as a prairie road.

"The scenery is finer than I ever saw on previous transcontinental trips. I doubt if Tumwater Canyon can be surpassed in this country. The Switchback over the Cascades is a wonderful piece of track, and worth a journey across the continent to see."—*Interview in St. Paul Dispatch with Vice-President Stevenson.*

78

Comin' 'Round the Bend

Once track was laid, crews were sent to build water towers, coal storage bins, and round houses for helper engines on either side of steep grades. In 1895, along the route of the Great Northern through the Marias Pass and along the Middle Fork of the Flathead River on the western slope of the Rockies, there were eleven water and coal stops and railroad yards or stations at Midvale (East Glacier), Summit, Bear Creek (Blacktail), Java, Essex, Nyack, and Belton (West Glacier). Settlements to house and feed the men who tended the round house, water tanks, and coal chutes grew up around these sidings. Populations increased when snow crews were brought in to clear tracks up and down the line. Some of these settlements became prosperous towns, whose populations peaked and waned with the tides of tourism and the logistics of changing railroad technology. The most immediately prosperous settlement growing up around the borders of Glacier was Belton at the western gateway to the mountains.

INSET: *Belton in its heyday, 1914. Belton Station at right with trellis and path leading to Belton Chalets.*
MARBLE PHOTO. COURTESY GLACIER NATIONAL PARK ARCHIVES

BELOW: *Eastbound Great Northern train pauses at Tunnel 40 along the Middle Fork of the Flathead River.*
COURTESY COLLECTION OF JOHN CHASE, GREAT FALLS, MT

Belton Station

When the work train moved down the line toward Kalispell in 1891, the railroad left two small box cars to serve as the Belton station. It would be a regular stop for trains traveling east and west. By the spring of 1892, Great Northern freight trains were running from St. Paul through to Spokane, and on August 14, 1892, through passenger train service was inaugurated.

The Flathead Valley west of Glacier was sparsely settled but its population was rapidly growing. The homesteads were producing grain and vegetables, and cattle and sheep grazed the rich grasslands. The railroad provided a means to get the products of these pioneer farmers to market. It also brought in

the first permanent families to Glacier. Charlie Howe, Milo Apgar, and Frank Geduhn built homes at the foot of Lake McDonald. A short time later Frank Geduhn moved to the head of the lake, and Denny Comeau, Frank Kelly, and George Snyder also built cabins there. They quickly discovered their land could not be successfully farmed. Some worked around Columbia Falls and Demersville to keep their homesteads going, and hunted game and trapped furs to sell for necessities.

While the few, hearty settlers were enjoying the fishing, hunting, and magnificent scenery of Glacier and trying to earn enough money to be able to stay there, F. I. Whitney, the Great Northern Railway's passenger and ticket agent in St. Paul, was distributing eloquent publicity booklets in the East about beautiful Lake McDonald as a tourist site. Around the same time, George Bird Grinnell's articles about the grandeur of the mountain lakes and streams and abundant wildlife and fish of the country were appearing in *The Century* and *Forest & Stream* magazines, joining accounts of Dr. Lyman Sperry's exploration of the mountains and glaciers to pique the interest of easterners in this remote wilderness. Tourists were discovering the Glacier area, and Belton became a busy railroad stop. The railroad settlement around the station began to grow. Edward Dow built a two-story hotel, a saloon, and a store and post office.

Milo Apgar and the other settlers quickly recognized the income potential of catering to the many tourists who got off the train here. He built rental cabins on his land at the foot of Lake McDonald, and his wife provided meals. The small village that grew up around them was known as Apgar. George Snyder had settled at the head of the lake and built a hotel. Visitors spent the night at Belton, then crossed the Middle Fork of the Flathead River in rowboats provided by Frank Kelly, Apgar, and Howe until a bridge was built in 1897. Then Dow, Snyder, and Apgar provided stage service between Belton and Lake McDonald. They

built crude roads around the lake to Snyder's Hotel. In 1898 Snyder began running a forty-foot steamboat to ferry tourists from Apgar to his hotel at the head of the lake.

By 1900 tourists, settlers, and investors were coming in great numbers. Ticket and baggage business at Belton outgrew its boxcar station and, around 1906, the railroad built a permanent depot west of the boxcars along the Great Northern track. The structure vaguely resembled the Swiss alpine chalet architecture that would later become the Great Northern theme for

BOTTOM: *Coaches lined up at Belton Depot, 1920.*
COURTESY GLACIER NATIONAL PARK ARCHIVES

BELOW: *Belton Station, 1920.*
COURTESY GLACIER NATIONAL PARK ARCHIVES

hotel and other structures throughout the park.

In 1909, Louis Hill, who had replaced his father James as head of the Great Northern, constructed the first of the many hotels and chalets he would build in the park. The Swiss-style hotel at Belton faced the Great Northern tracks and was linked to the Belton Station by a partially trellis-covered path. When the highway was built in 1932, the path from the station to the Belton Chalet was obliterated.

The Belton Station continues to serve as Amtrak's western rail entrance to Glacier National Park. Although the station maintains much of its original structure and styling, it has been re-roofed and some changes have been made over the years. The building also currently houses the Glacier Natural History Association headquarters and bookstore.

RIGHT: *Belton Station, 2003.*
STEPHEN PRINCE PHOTO

BELOW: *Tour group from Kalispell stops at Belton. The band is the Kalispell City Band under the direction of Marion B. Riffo. Belton Chalets are in the background.*
1912 KISER CO. PHOTO. COURTESY COLLECTION OF JOHN CHASE, GREAT FALLS, MT

MIDVALE (EAST GLACIER)

The eastern entrance to Glacier began as an unimpressive railroad siding on the Blackfeet Indian Reservation, which still included all of today's park. Until 1895, the vast number of tourists getting off the train at Belton to enjoy the scenery at Lake McDonald and the mountains beyond were actually trespassing on the Blackfeet reserve. Hill and the agents of the Great Northern had begun to realize the potential of this glaciered country for attracting railroad passengers. Along with the interests of the homesteaders, miners, and a surge of other ambitious exploiters there was strong support to reduce the size of the Blackfeet Reservation still further. Meanwhile the Indians were struggling with the white invasion from the west onto their reservation. They had neither the people nor the will to defend it. The acting Indian agent at Browning recommended to the Blackfeet that they sell the land to solve the trespass problem.

Thirty-five Blackfeet, including the once great but now elderly and tired warriors White Calf and Big Nose, met with United States commissioners in September 1895. The war-weary and conciliatory White Calf came to leadership among the Blackfeet in 1874. Big Nose, previously known as Three Suns, took

his place in the leadership in 1878, generally taking a position in favor of the old ways during councils. These two were among the leaders who had led the signing of the 1887 treaty agreeing to live on the reservation and ceding even more territory than had already been taken from them in the 1855, 1865, and 1877 treaties. During the 1895 meeting the two old warriors seemed to have switched sides. The normally conciliatory White Calf proclaimed the land valuable and asked for $3 million. After some discussion, Big Nose, in a reversal of his previous positions, announced that "We are to sell some land that is of little use to us.... If you wish to give a good price we will be pleased." After some more talk the Blackfeet accepted $1.5 million for the land that fifteen years later would become Glacier National Park.

Blackfeet Indians at Glacier Park Station.

GREAT NORTHERN RAILWAY COMPANY RECORDS. COURTESY MINNESOTA HISTORICAL SOCIETY

The railroad stop at the eastern entrance to Marias Pass was not within the land ceded by the 1895 treaty and remains a part of the Blackfeet Reservation. A small population of railroad people and settlers formed a town across the tracks from the Midvale station. When Louis Hill decided to locate the railway's headquarters hotel on the eastern side of Glacier after it became a park, he had Montana Senator Joseph Dixon put a bill through Congress for the United States to sell him 160 acres of reservation land, finally negotiated at $30 an acre.

In March 1912, within walking distance of the train station, Louis Hill began construction of the Glacier Park Hotel. A camp for workers was set up, and a spur laid off the main line to haul the 500- to 800-year-old trees from the Pacific coast forests used in the impressive 155-room structure. The hotel was opened on June 15, 1913.

The new Great Northern Railway Station at Midvale, probably taken in 1912. Upstairs windows have not been installed and construction materials are still scattered about. The large log at the left of the building remained there for many years. Photograph is from the album of Jean Juvik Bell whose grandfather was construction supervisor on the project.
COURTESY COLLECTION OF JOHN CHASE, GREAT FALLS, MT

Glacier Park Hotel.

PHOTO BY HILEMAN. GREAT NORTHERN RAILWAY COMPANY RECORDS. COURTESY MINNESOTA HISTORICAL SOCIETY

Summit

Some of the railroad stops between the eastern and western entrances to the park would disappear into history; some became ranger stations or headquarters for outfitters who lead tourists to wilderness campsites. Others prospered as tourist destinations.

The highest point of Marias Pass is 5,202 feet at Summit, Montana, where John Stevens spent that long, cold night atop the Divide when he discovered the lost pass. When the railroad was built, the Great Northern put a water tower and railroad yard on this spot. A sixty-foot turntable was installed in 1892 and, at various times, Summit had a tool house, agent house, section foreman's house, and telephone operator's car body. A depot was built in 1906. Then a second depot replacing the original structure was built in 1928 in the Great Northern's traditional alpine design. The new depot housed the agent's office, three living rooms, freight and baggage room, and a waiting room.

The Summit Station was relocated about a quarter mile southwest of its present location in 1985 and turned into a lodge.

William H. "Slippery Bill" Morrison was a well-known character among the settlers around Glacier, and legendary among railroad men. He was born in 1852 in Massachusetts. He made boilers for an engineering works in Connecticut then moved to Canada and worked as a powderman for the railroad. He went to work for the Great Northern sometime in the 1890s and lived in the rough and tumble, short-lived timber town of McCarthyville just west of the summit of Marias Pass.

When the Great Northern was building its line west they had sent Eugene McCarthy to locate timber for railroad ties. During his search for timber, McCarthy realized there

RIGHT: *Great Northern Railway's Summit section house and siding. Unpainted building to the left of the sign is "Slippery" Bill Morrison's place. The view is westbound. Circa 1920s.*
COURTESY COLLECTION OF JOHN CHASE, GREAT FALLS, MT

CENTER: *Jim Dickenson and Ha [sic] Lambert pose at Great Northern Railway Station at Summit, Montana. Early 1920s.*
PHOTOGRAPH BY J. R. BUHMILLER. COURTESY COLLECTION OF JOHN CHASE, GREAT FALLS, MT

BELOW: *Westbound passenger train meets freight at Summit. The open observation car was a glorious way to see the sights as the train made its way through the Rockies.*
COURTESY COLLECTION OF JOHN CHASE, GREAT FALLS, MT

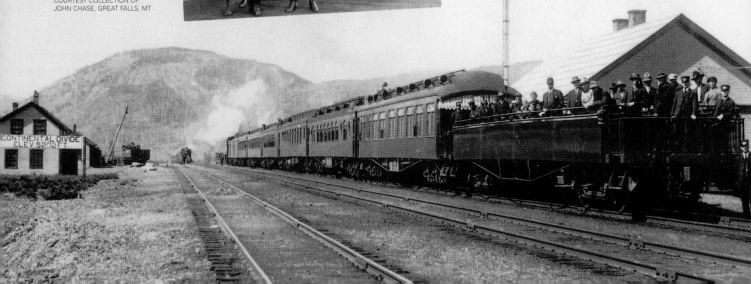

was only a small amount of land on the west slope of the Divide to establish a construction camp. Much to the Great Northern's chagrin and anger, he filed a Declaration of Occupancy and established a town site on that land. Under threat of court action, McCarthy compromised and a construction camp was built across Bear Creek from his McCarthyville town site. During the two years the town existed it had 1,000 people, a post office, hospital of sorts, and several saloons and gambling halls. It was known widely as the "toughest town in Montana." Newspapers reported that nearly ten percent of the population was buried in the town cemetery and that most of the deaths were due to gun fights. The town was slowly abandoned as railroad construction continued down the west slope. In 1921 most of the buildings burned when the wind came up while a section foreman for the railroad was burning ties.

William Morrison earned his nickname of "Slippery Bill" because he was able to spend an entire winter in McCarthyville and come out alive. Bill was a card player and staying above ground in that tough town as a gambler was no small feat. One night Bill was in one of the town's hastily built saloons, sitting on an old spike keg and playing cards at a makeshift table. That night he was a big winner. When he left the saloon to go home, some of the robbers who made up a big part of the McCarthyville transient population hit him on the head and searched his pockets. But Bill's winnings were not on him. The next morning, none the worse except for the lump on his head, Bill went back to the saloon, lifted the top off the spike keg he had been sitting on, took out his poker winnings and walked home.

When McCarthyville died, Bill bought a cabin on the summit of Marias Pass from woodcutters and acquired squatter's rights on 160 acres in the deal. He took a job running the Great Northern pay car that came once a month.

The Great Northern ran four passenger trains each day, and all had to stop at Summit

ABOVE: *Marias Pass in 1923. An eastbound Great Northern Railway freight waits in the siding at Summit. Note that there are no roads. Construction of U.S. Highway 2 along the southern border of Glacier National Park would not be completed until 1930.*
PHOTOGRAPH BY J. R. BUHMILLER. COURTESY COLLECTION OF JOHN CHASE, GREAT FALLS, MT

LEFT: *"Slippery Bill" Morrison, trainman and frontier philosopher. He became a legend among railroaders.*
COURTESY GLACIER NATIONAL PARK ARCHIVES

BELOW: *Old McCarthyville.*
COURTESY GLACIER NATIONAL PARK ARCHIVES

47

to test their air brakes and take on water for the old steam locomotives. Many passengers got off the train to stretch their legs and look around. Slippery Bill met the trains and took great pleasure in talking to visitors milling about the station. Slippery Bill was a great reader and frontier philosopher, and happy to expound on his theories to anyone who would listen. The wind blows almost continuously on the summit and, according to Pat Timmons, who had a job turning the locomotives around, Slippery Bill's long white whiskers never all blew the same way, half

blew one way and half blew the other. Bill was "a character" and well known among railroaders and locals. One day a woman got off the train and walked over to Bill. "My Lord, the wind sure blows around this place." "Yep, the most desolate place I ever saw in my life. Look at all the brush and shrubs around here and rocks as big as boxcars." The woman looked around then asked, "Where did all those rocks come from?"

"Lady, those rocks were washed down here by the glaciers."

"Glaciers! Where are the glaciers now?" she asked.

"Well," he said, "I'll tell you, lady, the glaciers have gone back after more rocks."

Slippery Bill Morrison died in 1932 at age eighty. He had donated part of his land for the sixty-foot-tall obelisk Theodore Roosevelt Memorial Monument constructed in 1931 at Summit, and the rest he willed to the federal government. A stone monument honoring Bill was placed next to the Roosevelt and John F. Stevens monuments. The three were relocated across the road from the original railroad yard in 1989.

RIGHT: *Newspaper clipping,* Missoulian, *May 21, 1891.*

BELOW RIGHT: *Theodore Roosevelt Memorial Monument.*
KERRY T. NICKOU PHOTO

INFESTED BY TOUGHS
McCarthysville on the Great Northern Railroad Extension

William Winters, the contractor, returned Tuesday from a visit to McCarthysville, which is on the line of the Great Northern railroad near the Marias Pass. In speaking of the town and its inhabitants to a Miner reporter yesterday, Mr. Winters said: "Do you see this old brown slouch hat I am wearing! Well, I am wearing it because when I went into the town of McCarthysville about two weeks ago I heard a couple of toughs remark that they guessed they would take a few shots at me and the stiff derby I was at that time wearing. That is a pretty tough town. Just the instant the people there caught sight of that stiff hat they wanted to scrap with me, and they kept up their lick until I had to change it. I don't wear that hat again in that country. The town contains about 150 people, who support twenty saloons, eight houses of ill-fame and two grocery stores. It is a great place for [Italians], who are being shipped there from the east now to work on the railroad. At Two Medicine, a little town twenty-two miles from McCarthys-ville, the [Italians] came very near having a riot a few days ago. A whole gang of them were congregated in a saloon discussing the best and most feasible plan of getting even with the American people for the killing of the members of the Mafia at New Orleans, when one of them accidently shot a companion, wounding him severely. Then a friend of the wounded man, supposing it had been done on purpose, pulled a gun and shot the shooter, when he in turn was shot by a friend of the second man shot. Then a big [Italian] rose up from a corner and shot the last shooter, which put a quietus on the proceedings, although affairs looked threatening for a while. Work on the road is progressing slowly, about two miles of track being laid each day. I have two gangs working. No, sir: this old brown hat is good enough for me the next time I go there."

Missoulian   May 21, 1891

ESSEX/WALTON

Eastbound trains needed help getting over the summit of Marias Pass. The steepest grade began sixteen miles west of the summit. There the Great Northern constructed a railroad yard to house the helper engines necessary to pull the eastbound freights over the grade from the western slope. The yard was named Essex, probably for one of the railroaders, and then changed to "Walton" in 1926 when many Great Northern Railway stations were renamed to promote Glacier country's historical lore. Walton was named for the famous bait and fly fisherman Izaak Walton, who wrote *The Compleat Angler* in 1653, a book still considered the fisherman's bible. Later, the town would take back its original name of Essex and the Izaak Walton Inn would continue to be a tribute to the old fisherman.

The Great Northern put up three water tanks and a coal tower to fill the big Mallets and 2-10-2s used as pusher engines on the grade. They built a four-stall engine house and an eighty-foot turntable, a section house and a generating plant. Seven helper engine crews were stationed there. Heavy snowfalls and frequent avalanches up and down the line required at least two and often as many as nine snow service gangs to continuously shovel snow off the tracks onto flatcars for dumping into Bear Creek. In 1907 the yard was enlarged. A Y-track was constructed, a portable depot was brought in, and a boarding house was built. In 1910 a double track was run from Essex to Summit.

BOTTOM: *Essex, Montana, in the Rocky Mountains. In the land of snow. Early 1900s.*
COURTESY STUMPTOWN HISTORICAL SOCIETY, WHITEFISH, MT

BELOW: *Station at Essex built in the late 1920s. It was the third building to serve as the Great Northern Station at Essex, Montana. The first was a standard two-story section house.*
PHOTOGRAPH BY JOHN CHASE. COURTESY COLLECTION OF JOHN CHASE, GREAT FALLS, MT

ABOVE: *Chuck Welch drawing of the Izaak Walton Inn and Essex Depot, July 1983.*
COURTESY OF LARRY AND LYNDA VIELLEUX, IZAAK WALTON INN, ESSEX, MT

BELOW: *Great Northern Railway brochure.*
COURTESY JOHN CHASE COLLECTION AND
BURLINGTON-NORTHERN-SANTA FE RAILWAY

A small beanery built in 1909 was purchased by the Great Northern to serve as an eating facility for their crews. The restaurant burned down in 1918 and another was built the following year. This last beanery was painted the same color as the red on the Great Northern insignia and became known as the Red Beanery. It burned in 1935.

The railroad workers, some quartered in tents and abandoned railroad cars, sent in numerous petitions demanding permanent housing. I. E. Manion, the superintendent at Whitefish, took up their cause. In 1937 he wrote to the general manager of the Great Northern: "With as many as eight or nine crews working out of Walton in snow service, with three helper engine crews and various officers, including roadmasters, trainmasters, traveling engineer, and master mechanic, also master carpenter frequently tying up at that point, the hotel should be of sufficient size to accommodate six crews of five men each tying up at one time, and three or four Division officers and accommodations for the necessary hotel help."

On April 28, 1939, the Great Northern entered into a contract with Addison Miller, which allowed his company to build and operate a hotel and lunchroom on railroad land at Walton. The Izaak Walton Inn opened in November 1939. It had twenty-nine guest rooms, ten bathrooms, a lobby, dining room, kitchen, general store, with a recreation room and bar in the basement.

At the time, there were plans to open up the Park Creek country just north of Walton to more tourism, and the hotel was designed to serve as the middle entrance to the park in addition to housing and feeding Great Northern crews. World War II halted the plan, and the middle entrance to Glacier National Park never materialized. However, over the years the inn became a favorite of park visitors and cross-country skiers, anglers, and hikers out to enjoy the surrounding wilderness. Filled with railroad memorabilia, it is a popular stop for railroad enthusiasts. Its front porch and dining room face the yard and main railroad line where the successor to the Great Northern, the Burlington, Northern and Santa Fe, continues to run freight, and Amtrak brings passenger trains from the east and west.

Go Great to Glacier...Go
GREAT NORTHERN RAILWAY

The Trainmen

When railroading was king, the men who made the trains go were revered much as the cowboy of western lore, and the daring test pilot and the adventurous astronaut of today. They were more than mere mortals. They controlled powerful machines speeding to distant places over miles of barren desert, dangerous mountains, and narrow wobbling bridges. They pushed their machines through rock slides, blizzards, avalanches, floods, wildfires and, for a time, attacks by hostile Indians and ruthless train robbers. In the 1890s, engineers on most lines had locomotives assigned to them and they took personal pride in the power and appearance of their engines. The wail of the train whistle was distinctive. The people who lived in the towns along the line knew the whistle and knew the engineer. No matter where he came from he was a local hero on his way to far-off places. Small boys dreaming of adventure yearned to be railroad engineers. The rumbling of the wheels, clanking of the couplers, the lonesome whistle blowing, the engine bell ringing called many a young man away from home and hearth to become a trainman. The image of the trainman was immortalized in such songs as *Casey Jones, John Henry,* and the *Wreck of the Old 97* and in various stage plays: the 1867 stage play *Under the Gaslight,* the 1896 movie *The Great Train Robbery,* and the 1899 play *The Fast Mail.* Just as with the image of the cowboy, the heroic trainmen appeared in magazines and dime novels shooting it out with Indians and train robbers, or taking their trains over crumbling, flood-ravaged bridges.

The romantic image of the trainmen did grow from the seeds of reality. Much of what is in song, stage, and novel, and later in motion pictures, did happen, at least in part. In 1900 Engineer Casey Jones left Memphis headed to Canton, Mississippi, on the Cannon Ball Express. He was determined to make up

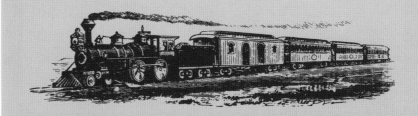

Casey Jones

Come all you rounders if you want to hear,
A story 'bout a brave engineer.
Casey Jones was the rounder's name,
On a six eight wheeler, boys, he won his fame.

Casey Jones, mounted to the cabin.
Casey Jones, orders in his hand,
Casey Jones, mounted to the cabin,
And he took his fare-well trip to the promised land.

"Put in your water and shovel in your coal,
Put your head out the window, watch them drivers roll,
I'll run her till she leaves the rail,
'Cause I'm eight hours late with that western mail."
He looked at his watch and his watch was slow,
He looked at the water and the water was low,
He turned to the fireman and then he said,
"We're goin' to reach Frisco but we'll be dead."

Casey pulled up that Reno Hill,
He tooted for the crossing with an awful shrill,
The Switchman knew by the engine's moan
That the man at the throttle was Casey Jones,
He pulled up within two miles of the place
Number four stared him right in the face,
He turned to the fireman, said, "Boy you better jump
'Cause there's two locomotives that's a-goin' to bump."

Casey said just before he died,
"There's two more roads that I'd like to ride."
The fireman said, "what could they be?"
"The Southern Pacific and the Santa fe."
Mrs. Casey sat on her bed a-sighin',
Just received a message that Casey was dyin'
Said. "Go to bed, children, and hush your cryin',
'Cause you got another papa on the Salt Lake Line."

Seibert & Newton, 1909

ABOVE: *Train crews pose alongside a Great Northern Railway Class F-9 2-8-0 helper locomotive at Summit, Montana, in 1923. The engine was built by Alco-Brooks in 1903 and rebuilt as a Class C-3 in 1925.*
PHOTOGRAPH BY J. R. BUHMILLER. COURTESY COLLECTION OF JOHN CHASE, GREAT FALLS, MT

BELOW: *Engineer L. O. Hileman and operator A. O. Therriault pose in front of their Class F-9 2-8-0 locomotive used in helper service up Marias Pass.*
COURTESY COLLECTION OF JOHN CHASE, GREAT FALLS, MT

for lost time. Just as the highballing train neared Vaughn, the fireman saw the caboose of a freight train ahead. Casey shouted to the fireman to jump, but Casey was still in the cab when it smashed into the rear of the freight. The story of John Henry, that steel-driving man, who declared "Before your steam drill beats me down, I'll hammer my fool self to death" may have been dramatized but it was based on an 1870s event in Virginia. When a steam drill was brought in to replace a number of workers, a contest between man and machine was staged to prove which was faster, and John Henry was given the job.

In their day trainmen were a heroic lot, and they earned their image in a time and culture when a man's measure was taken by his deeds and the level of hardship he endured to accomplish them. Trainmen's lives were adventures of immeasurable hardships. They worked grueling hours driven by rigid schedules and plagued by the dangers of their profession: broken or missing rails, trees or boulders across the tracks, damaged bridges, wash-outs, avalanches, and wrecks. Then, too, they faced endless hours of boredom as the locomotives

churned uneventfully across miles of prairie. The men were semi-homeless, not knowing from one day to the next where they might be. The work was hard and it was dangerous, yet they would trade their life for no other. Trainmen, like the brotherhood of soldiers, were linked by hardship and pinned by pride, strength of purpose, and railroad humor.

In 1888 nearly 2,000 men were killed and over 20,000 men were injured railroading in the nation. In 1891, when the Great Northern was winding its way through Marias Pass on its way to the Flathead Valley, the relative numbers had not changed much, but by 1905, with the advent of improved technologies and safety laws, the rate of occupational accidents began to drop.

Early railroaders dealt with inherent risks in nearly all the jobs. The switchman, who had the tricky job of fastening a train together with link-and-pin couplings, risked his fingers and his life. He pushed one end of the link, an iron loop like that of a huge chain, into a slot in the drawbar of a car and fastened it by shoving the pin, an iron spike, through the hole in the drawbar. The other end of the link was fastened in the same way to the car being coupled. The riskiest part came when a link was disengaged from one car. When the link dropped for whatever reason, the switchman stepped between the cars, lifted the hanging link and guided it into the other car. When the cars were moving the switchman ran between the cars, keeping his feet out from under rolling wheels and clear of switching points on the track. Often the drawbars of two cars being coupled were set at different heights, as were their heavy beam bumpers. The switchman used gooseneck links to compensate for the difference in height, but it was not uncommon for one bumper beam to slide over the other while the switchman was busy wrestling with the link and pin, crushing him to death—many a switchman met that fate.

The brakeman's life was no better. The very early railroads used hand brakes that were manipulated by iron wheels on the roofs of the cars. The brakemen, usually two to a train, rode on top. When the engineer whistled for brakes, one brakeman started from the front of the train and the other from the end of the train. They hurriedly worked toward the center, setting the brakes, jumping from one swaying car

ABOVE: *Photographer John Chase has his picture taken in the cab of No. 2518. This was a Class P-2 4-8-2 locomotive and the power on the westbound Oriental Limited in 1948.*
COURTESY COLLECTION OF JOHN CHASE, GREAT FALLS, MT

LEFT: The Freight Train Brakeman *by O. V. Schubert. A romanticized drawing of the brakeman struggling in a blizzard to bring a freight to a stop.*
COURTESY CULVER PICTURES

to the next. A particular hazard to the brakeman was the weather. He rode on top through freezing rain and blizzards, jumping from one ice-coated slippery car to the next. If he survived the winters, he faced the summers when the blazing sun heated the rooftops to scorching levels. As more powerful locomotives and faster trains came onto the lines, the brakeman's job grew more intense and dangerous.

By the time the Great Northern reached Montana, life for switchmen and brakemen was a little easier. Automatic couplers and the air brake had been invented in 1868 but it was not until 1893 that they became mandatory. However, many of the railroads were slow to order the newer equipment and make the conversion. Some railroads did not have the new couplers or airbrakes until as late as 1900.

Even with improved brakes, taking a train through the mountains was hazardous. One of the great fears was air leaks that could render the brakes useless on the steep grades. Checking the air was a sacred routine but not always foolproof.

In 1901, one of the Great Northern's worst accidents up to that time happened near Nyack. A twenty-eight-car freight train headed east stopped at Essex for water and coal. The lead locomotive was uncoupled and went to the water tower leaving the helper engine in the rear to hold the train. The engineer of the helper engine set the air brakes and left the engine. The air leaked and the train began to slip backward, picking up speed on the steep hill. Before the crew could get to the runaway train, it was speeding down the hill at 75 to 100 miles per hour. As the runaway sped by the switch at Nyack, it struck a caboose and day coach on the siding, wrecking them and starting a fire when the oil lamps in the caboose ignited. A few hundred feet farther down the line it overtook a westbound passenger train,

Photographs of train wrecks near Glacier National Park, 1907–1971.
COURTESY STUMPTOWN HISTORICAL SOCIETY, WHITEFISH, MT

slamming full force into it and buckling the train into a disastrous wreck. The fire on the siding was fierce and flames were burning their way toward the wrecked trains. Ten cars of shingles were at the rear of the freight. When the freight hit the passenger train, shingles were thrown all over the wrecked passenger cars. The fire reached the wreck, igniting the shingles, and walls of flames engulfed the cars, the brush, and the telephone poles alongside the track. Men in the day coach on the rear of the train got the worst of it. They were from Duluth, going to work on the Jennings branch of the Great Northern. Thirty-four died and thirteen were injured. The rear sleeper could not be saved although it had not left the track, but its occupants were hurried into forward cars and pulled ahead out of the reach of the fire.

In the line of progression to the position of heroic locomotive engineer, a man had to serve his time as fireman. The fireman's job was a coveted position for all its hardships. It took brute strength. Early engines burned up to as much as 200 pounds of coal per mile depending on the grade and speed. When the train was highballing, a fireman might have to shovel the coal into the firebox at rates of two tons every half hour and spread the coal around in the box to keep the fire hot. In addition to the back-breaking, blackening work of keeping the firebox filled, the fireman also had the tricky, hazardous job of oiling the cylinders of the fast-moving locomotive. When the sliding valves above a locomotive's steam cylinders needed oiling, the fireman climbed out on the running boards of the moving train, made his way carefully alongside the hot boiler, and poured liquid tallow from a long-spouted can onto the valves. This most dreaded duty was relieved when a device that mixed oil and boiler water—creating steam

Photographs of train wrecks near Glacier National Park,
1907–1971.

with its own lubricant—was put on locomotives in the 1880s.

Despite the improvements made in locomotives, taking a train over the Rockies, even on the low grades of Marias Pass, was inherently dangerous. On steep downgrades, free-running cars were likely to coast faster than the engine could run and still hold the rails. There are numerous accounts of trains careening over the embankments. As tragic as some have been, such as the runaway train at Essex, some of the accounts have a humorous twist.

In November 1914, the car next to the caboose jumped the track a few miles east of Belton. It rolled down the seventy-five-foot embankment and landed right-side-up in the river. In its roll down the mountain, the roof was torn off and 128 boxes of apples broke apart and floated down the river. For some time after the accident it was a common sight to see homesteaders fishing for apples instead of trout. One enterprising man drove his team out and gathered apples with a fish net.

Sometime after World War II, a westbound train was coming down Essex Hill from Summit when a snow slide hit it just behind the engine, sliding under the train and derailing several cars. One was a tank car loaded with Karo syrup and the other a boxcar loaded with stationery for the Rexall stores in Seattle. The tank car smashed through the box car, rupturing its tank of syrup and crushing and bursting open the cartons of stationery in the box car. Both cars rolled down the bank, thousands of gallons of syrup mixing with tons of paper. It was in winter and cold, and the syrup thick. The mess was impossible to clean up in these conditions. Railroad officials decided to wait until spring when conditions were better. Much to the amusement of the crews and passengers, every train going by for several weeks could look down on a gathering of smeared, paper-plastered, bears gulping down sweetened wads of paper. According to the late Frank

A ROTARY CLEARING THE TRACKS OF THE G.N. RAILWAY AFTER THE SNOW SLIDES IN THE ROCKY MOUNTAINS. FIELDING. MONT. JAN. 1911.

PIEGAN PASS

Gregg, the Stumptown Historical Society historian who provided this story, the bears' ridiculous appearance didn't seem to bother them at all.

Stories that become part of railroad lore often are those describing the calm dispatch with which the engineer handles near-death situations. Some have been immortalized in songs like *Casey Jones* and *The Wreck of the Number Nine*. Some, like these from the Stumptown archives and printed in Walter Sayre's *Looking Back: Whimsical Whitefish Through the Years*, add to the lore.

A short distance east of Belton (the date was not recorded), engineer Charles Buckley was at the throttle when his engine and two cars derailed. He blew the whistle signaling the trainmen to jump. The locomotive rolled down the bank and landed in the Middle Fork of the Flathead River. After an anxious search, rescuers found all the trainmen except Buckley. Finally, after they had looked everywhere they thought he could have jumped or fallen to, they went down the bank to the river to investigate the half-submerged locomotive. There they found the missing engineer, sitting on the pilot (cow catcher) of the machine calmly fishing.

Around this same period, Silas Schutt's locomotive left the tracks near Essex and rolled down to the river, turning over and over several times. Schutt went with it and was found almost unhurt in the cab. His rescuers asked him why he did not blow the whistle.

"I did," he said, "every time the top was up."

In a train crew the conductor was the captain of the train. He supervised the other trainmen, took passengers' tickets, kept track of the schedule, saw to loading and unloading luggage, and signaled the engineer when to start the train moving. His job included keeping unruly passengers in line and called for the ultimate in diplomacy. The conductor was always handsomely dressed and carried the trademark of his profession—a heavy gold watch chain attached to the large gold watch in his pocket, which he frequently consulted. He was responsible if something, if anything, went wrong on the train and he was the trainmen best known to the passengers. His "All aboard" signaled the beginning of their journey, and they would see him at his duties all along the way.

Conductor calls the "All aboard" in a Great Northern photo.

COURTESY GLACIER NATIONAL PARK ARCHIVES AND BURLINGTON-NORTHERN-SANTA FE RAILWAY

"All Aboard"

THE *Empire Builder*

Air-conditioned observation and dining cars are only one of the many features that make travel on the Empire Builder a pleasure trip. This famous transcontinental train leaves Chicago every evening, pauses to pick up more passengers at St. Paul and Minneapolis next morning, then glides smoothly westward toward Glacier National Park, Spokane, Seattle, Tacoma and Portland. At the same time another Empire Builder leaves Portland, Tacoma and Seattle nightly for the eastward journey to Spokane, the Twin Cities and Chicago.

For more than 1600 miles this luxurious train is hauled by locomotives using electricity or oil for power. They take the train up grade without huffing and puffing, down grade without racing. Powerful enough to maintain a uniform speed, these locomotives and the train itself are also given the advantage of a magnificent road-bed from

which sharp curves and grades have been eliminated, even in the mountains. Thus you cross the Rocky Mountain and the Cascade ranges without being conscious of effort.

You relish Empire Builder meals. You sleep exceptionally well. You meet worthwhile people. You find courteous, friendly service eager to anticipate your wishes. You soon discover that the Empire Builder provides everything in the way of "creature comforts" . . . solarium lounge, library, radio lounge, buffet lounge, men's and women's smoking rooms, barber, valet, baths, drawing rooms and compartments en suite or separately, and Pullman single sections.

Should you wish to travel most economically, this train also provides comfortable coaches and tourist sleeping cars. Here indeed is an extra fine train, running over an extra fine route, without extra fare.

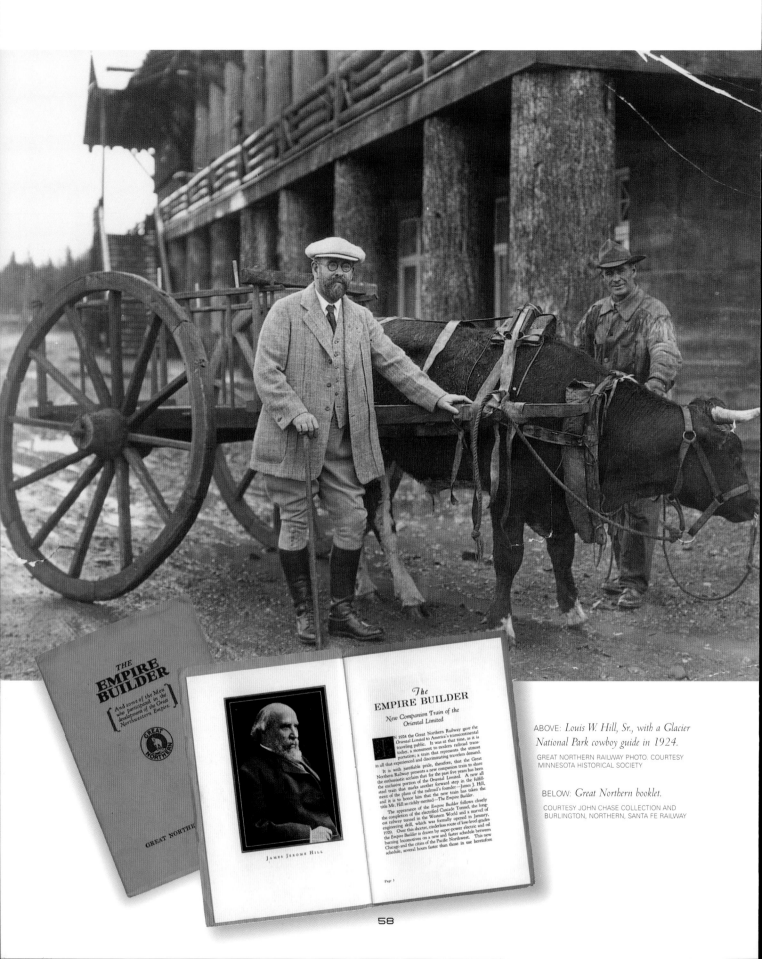

ABOVE: *Louis W. Hill, Sr., with a Glacier National Park cowboy guide in 1924.*

GREAT NORTHERN RAILWAY PHOTO. COURTESY MINNESOTA HISTORICAL SOCIETY

BELOW: *Great Northern booklet.*

COURTESY JOHN CHASE COLLECTION AND BURLINGTON, NORTHERN, SANTA FE RAILWAY

CHAPTER 5

LAST OF THE EMPIRE BUILDERS

Most men who have really lived have had, in some shape, their great adventure. The railway is mine.

—James J. Hill

James Hill had built an empire. He had battled with the railroad giants of his day and beat them at their game. In 1893, when the last spike of his transcontinental railroad was driven, the other railroads of the country were in financial trouble. His closest rival—Henry Villard's Northern Pacific Railroad—had fallen into receivership. Hill pounced on this opportunity. He worked with New York banker J. P. Morgan, outmaneuvered Edward Henry Harriman of the Union Pacific, and quietly gained control of the Northern Pacific in 1901.

During this same period Hill was pushing to strengthen his railroad systems in the east by acquiring the very profitable Chicago, Burlington & Quincy Railroad. The Burlington threatened Harriman's lines, and Harriman and Hill battled for control. Hill fought Harriman to a draw. It was one of many battles of these two lions of the railroads. Harriman acquired the North Coast Railroad with lines from the Columbia River into Hill's territory—Puget Sound. Hill countered by invading Harriman's territory. Hill's Great Northern and Northern Pacific announced joint incorporation of the Portland & Seattle Railway Company that linked Spokane and Portland. The Portland & Seattle acquired the Astoria & Columbia

Great Northern brochure.
COURTESY JOHN CHASE COLLECTION AND BURLINGTON, NORTHERN, SANTA FE RAILWAY

River Railroad, which had lines from Portland to the Columbia and down the Oregon coast to Seaside.

Hill's lines would go on to build the North Bank Road, and acquire the Oregon Trunk Line and Oregon Electric Railway. Harriman's Union Pacific acquired the Yellowstone Park Railroad Company and extended lines east along the Snake River from Riparia, Washington, to Lewiston, Idaho. The Hill–Harriman battles weaved a massive system of railroad lines throughout the Northwest. Towns emerged, farmers prospered, and industry thrived. In 1909, Standard Oil's Chicago, Milwaukee & St. Paul Railroad added to the tapestry of tracks in the Northwest.

In 1907, the sixty-nine-year-old lion was ready to "relax the bonds of duty and labor." James J. Hill turned the leadership of his vast empire over to the son he had trained for fourteen years to take his place—Louis W. Hill. James resigned as president of the Great Northern and became chairman of the board. Louis was elected president. James Hill may have relaxed the bonds of duty; however, he did not retire. He used his still tremendous energy to continue battling with Harriman for the rest of Oregon and into California. Hill died in 1916 shortly before his lines reached San Francisco.

The life work of James Hill is legendary. He had battled the best of his kind into submission, and he did what they could not—build a successful transcontinental railroad without government assistance. Along the way he populated the Northwest, and built an empire laced with tracks and dotted with fields of wheat, roaming cattle, granaries, industrial plants, centers of trade, small towns, and growing metropolises. He was praised as the "Empire Builder" and cursed as the "Little Giant," "Red River Pirate," and "Oregon Bandit." Farmers and ranchers swore by him or against him depending on their circumstances. A common frontier oath was "By Jesus H. Kee-ryst and Jim Jam Hill" but, conversely, Harvard University named a chair in railroad economics in his honor. Whether history finds that what he did was good or bad for the country, he was one of the great men of his time.

Louis Warren Hill grew up in the shadow of the man and the legend. But Louis was intelligent enough to realize he could not

Glacier National Park ad.

COURTESY JOHN CHASE COL-
LECTION AND BURLINGTON,
NORTHERN, SANTA FE RAILWAY

replace such a man. "There was not room in one family for more than one Empire Builder," he said. He could only do for his father's railroad what he could do best and make his own imprint on the empire.

Louis was born in May 1872. He had two brothers and seven sisters, but he was the child most interested in their father's railroads. He was educated at Yale and at twenty-one began working his way up the Great Northern ladder through various positions until, at age thirty-five, he became president of the line.

Louis had witnessed the effect of the volumes of brochures, timetables, posters, and other promotional articles in bringing freight and passengers to all railroads, and particularly the very successful promotional work of Great Northern passenger agent F. I. Whitney. Louis Hill was more interested in advertising than he was in operating the railroad and he was talented in public relations. He left the operations of the Great Northern to his able assistant Ralph Budd, and began the campaign that would put his own mark on the northwest.

Although as early as the late 1880s, railroads recognized the tourist potential of the northwest and began issuing brochures extolling the "gorgeous scenery of the Rockies," the "stately palisades of the Columbia" and the health benefits of the "sun, the mountain breeze, the crisp, mild air, which combine to invigorate and heal," the Northwest was slow to become a favorite tourist destination. Most of the area was still isolated and lacked the comforts that wealthy easterners enjoyed in other recreational Meccas. All the transcontinentals launched colorful and effective advertising, but the Great Northern's promotional campaigns would be considered the star of railroad public relations.

Shortly after the Great Northern's last spike was driven, its passenger agents began writing eloquent brochures and timetables that enticed travelers to take the Great Northern to the Northwest. In 1894 they wrote "that Lake McDonald is destined to become a famous resort in itself for its fishing, hunting, scenic and health-giving attractions" and went on to describe the other scenic wonders along the line of the railroad proclaiming "every rod forward presents new scenes, from merely picturesque to exalted and sublime and one constantly feels with each that no other can furnish so fair and grand a sight." In 1901, the agents announced "that nowhere in America can such a combination of climate, comfort and scenery be found as amongst the great mountains on the line of the Great Northern Railway." These brochures and timetables described the country from St. Paul to Puget Sound. It wasn't until Louis Hill took over management of the railroad that the Great Northern found its keystone of advertising, one that would transcend its own existence—Glacier National Park.

RIGHT: *Great Northern Railway/Glacier National Park brochure.*
COURTESY GLACIER NATIONAL PARK ARCHIVES
AND BURLINGTON-NORTHERN-SANTA FE RAILWAY

BELOW: *Lake McDonald.*
VALLEY, PLAIN & PEAK: SCENES ALONG THE LINE OF THE GREAT NORTHERN,
GREAT NORTHERN 1894 BOOKLET; COURTESY K. ROSS TOOLE ARCHIVES,
UNIVERSITY OF MONTANA, MISSOULA

LAKE McDONALD lies on the western side of the Montana Rockies, two miles from Belton Station. The lake is eighteen miles long and from one to three miles wide, set like a grand Kohinoor in the midst of Alpine grandeur.

McDonald is destined to become a famous resort in itself for its fishing, hunting, scenic, and health-giving attractions, and come in for a full share of poetic inspiration in verse and artistic reproduction on canvas. Six miles from its head is another lake in the cleft rock, several miles in length, and near by is a vast icy field, covering many square miles, as grand and imposing as any Swiss glacier, and much easier to reach. There are other lakes and glaciers and wonderful sights in this mighty region.

"With every scenic feature that makes the Alpine lakes attractive, with a far greater variety of game and fish, and immunity from the petty exactions of fees and tolls which make traveling in Switzerland vexatious, it is destined to become the leading resort in America as soon as it becomes widely known. Already its annual visitors are counted by scores. Its accommodations are more ample and comfortable than the primitive hostelries at Saranac and St. Regis, in the Adirondacks were, and the promise of a more brilliant history than theirs is before it."— *Charles Hallock in the American Angler.*

52

Great Northern buffet/library/observation car.

VALLEY, PLAIN & PEAK: SCENES ALONG THE LINE OF THE GREAT NORTHERN,
GREAT NORTHERN 1894 BOOKLET, COURTESY K. ROSS TOOLE ARCHIVES, UNIVERSITY OF MONTANA, MISSOULA

CHAPTER 6

GILDED AND GOLDEN

The vast wealth produced in the United States from 1878 through 1889 created a showy, opulent way of life among the rich. Humorist Mark Twain ridiculed the lifestyle, calling this period of the industrial era "The Gilded Age." By the 1880s the Gilded Age was peaking and the golden age of passenger train travel beginning. Great fortunes were made. Among them were John D. Rockefeller in oil, Andrew Carnegie in steel, and the transcontinental railroad barons such as Thomas Scott of the Pennsylvania and Union Pacific, Leland Stanford, Charles Crocker, Collis Huntington, and Mark Hopkins of the Central Pacific, and Edward Harriman of the Union Pacific. James J. Hill and the men he had deals with along his journey to build an empire were growing rich as well. The production of iron and steel was at an all-time high. Waves of immigrants were working in factories, mines and on farms. The West's lumber, gold, silver, copper, and wheat were plucked from the earth, and trains steamed across the country in ever increasing numbers, moving the goods of the resource-rich West to the factory-filled East.

The "gilded" vacationed in Europe and at luxurious resorts throughout the East. Railroads had successfully lured immigrants to the West to fill the empty space with farms and towns, using a flood of posters, pamphlets, and books extolling the resources that awaited them in the vast emptiness of the frontier. The growing number of wealthy

Great Northern Railway 1928 booklet.
COURTESY GLACIER NATIONAL PARK ARCHIVES
AND BURLINGTON-NORTHERN-SANTA FE RAILWAY

tourists offered a new source of revenue. In addition to appealing to investors and immigrants to come west, railroad advertising in the early 1880s began to target the wealthy tourists, seeking to lure them away from Europe and the East and to the wonders of the West.

At this same time, the nation's natural resources were being exploited in every corner of the land, but public support to protect water, timber, minerals, and unique natural scenery was gaining momentum. The nation was becoming aware of the devastating results of unchecked use. Grassroots movements to protect the country's resources for the future actually began as early as 1832, when the hot springs of Arkansas were regarded as important enough to the nation's heritage to be protected from development and set aside as a national reserve. Other efforts at conservation of natural resources and unique American landscapes were proposed in ensuing years without much support in a country just beginning to realize its potential as an industrial giant, and consuming its resources with abandon. However, in the 1860s, Frederick Law Olmsted put up a successful fight for preservation of Yosemite's "natural scenes of impressive character." Congress gave the area to the State of California to be set aside as "a park for public use," thus establishing precedent for withdrawing land from private use and forming the park concept. In 1872, Yellowstone was established as the nation's first national park.

California's Sequoia, General Grant, and Yosemite areas became parks in 1890, and Washington's Mount Rainier in 1899. Two years later, the passionate outdoorsman Theodore Roosevelt became president and twisted Congressional arms to put more money into preservation programs. His enthusiastic rhetoric energized the Congress and the country.

The great outdoors was popular. Five additional national parks were created in the West in the following six years: Crater Lake in Oregon, the caverns of Wind Cave near the Black Hills, Sullys' Hill in North Dakota (now a wildlife refuge), Platt in southern Oklahoma, and Mesa Verde pueblo archeological sites in Colorado.

The railroads were very much a part of the movement to create these national parks. They had for years promoted the known scenic wonders along their right-of-ways to lure immigrants and tourists to the West. The potential of national parks to generate passengers for their lines seemed obvious. Creating such parks was an increasingly popular movement that gave these natural wonders status and national recognition. Wealthy easterners who vacationed in Europe and the eastern resorts would be enticed to take the trains to the scenic marvels of the American West.

The railroads encouraged various groups to submit bills proposing national park status for places that could be reached from their lines, and spoke out strongly in favor of these bills when they came before Congressional committees. The Southern Pacific lobbied for California's Yosemite, Sequoia, and General Grant national parks and Oregon's Crater Lake National Park. The Atchison, Topeka & Santa Fe pushed for the protection of the Grand Canyon, which was finally set aside as a national monument by order of Theodore Roosevelt in 1908. The Northern Pacific was already enjoying the advantage of having a line near Yellowstone National Park, which had been established in 1872. Yellowstone's geysers could be reached by stage from the main line in Livingston, some fifty-four miles from the park border. James Hill had taken control of the Northern Pacific in 1901 and put in a branch line from Livingston to the border in 1903 to handle the growing popularity of Yellowstone as a tourist destination. Edward Harriman, who was still locked in combat with Hill for Union Pacific territory, also put in a branch line from St. Anthony, Idaho, to Yellowstone in 1908.

At the top of the country, the Great Northern's tracks ran along the southern border of great mountains, lakes, streams, and—

"Here is where God sat when he made America."

—an unknown packer sitting on the shores of Lake McDonald

A 1912 Great Northern brochure eloquently described the country it bordered:

"Here the Rocky Mountains tumble and froth like a wind-whipped tide as they career off to the northwest of Canada and Alaska. Here is the backbone of the continent and the little and big beginning of things; here, huddled close together, are tiny streams the span of a hand in width, that, leagues away to the north, the south and the west flow mighty rivers into Hudson's Bay, the Gulf of Mexico and the Pacific Ocean; here peak after peak, named and unnamed, rear their saw-tooth edges to the clouds; three-score glaciers within its borders are slowly and silently grinding away at their epochal task; three hundred lakes in valley and in mountain pocket give back to the sky its blue, gray or green; half a thousand waterfalls cascade from everlasting snow in misty torrents or milk-white traceries; rainbows flicker and vanish in the ever changing play waters, while the clear Montana sun does tricks of light and shade on pine and rock. High up on some gale-swept crag the shy goat pauses for a moment and plunges from view; lower down the big horn sheep treads his sure-footed way; the dreaded silver-tip prowl sullenly in the upper reaches of the timber; the clownish black bear shuffles to his huckleberry patch; far up in the blue, between mountain and sun, the bald eagle sails his rounded periods peering down for the timid creature beneath the leaves and the shadows of the rocks. And all is as it was when the world's first day was done, save for some man tracks here and there on the winding slopes."

as unique in America as the geysers of Yellowstone—the glaciers of northern Montana. But as late as 1907, this scenic wonderland was not a national park.

The region was, however, a forest reserve. The reserves were established to protect timber resources but did not have the protective status of national parks and did not prevent hunting, mining, or settlement. In 1897, President Grover Cleveland established the Flathead and Lewis and Clark forest reserves in northern Montana. The Flathead Forest Reserve included what would become Glacier National Park. Marias Pass and the Great Northern tracks separated the two reserves. A trifling amount of government funds were allocated to protect the resources of the reserves and little was done until 1901 when Theodore Roosevelt became president.

Teddy Roosevelt, known as the conservation president, used his soft voice and big stick to persuade Congress to authorize funds to hire forest range riders (rangers) to patrol and enforce the provisions of the reserves. The forest rangers were hired on to "look for fires, timber thieves, squatters and game violators." They worked for $60 a month, provided their own board and horses, and patrolled vast areas of wilderness. Frank Liebig, the first ranger in the area that would become Glacier National Park, patrolled the entire area from Belton to the Canadian border—over a half million acres—from 1902 until 1910. Liebig and the other forest rangers were diligent in their duties and did everything they were authorized to do. Establishing the forest reserves was a step in the right direction, but it did not protect scenic beauty as would national park status.

Author and naturalist George Bird Grinnell had explored the valleys and mountains of Glacier in 1885 and coined the phrase "Crown of the Continent" in a 1900 article for *Century* magazine. As owner and editor of *Forest and Stream*, he often described the wonders of this country, bringing it to national attention. He

also used magazines to promote preservation of the area's natural resources. In 1907, Grinnell and well-known lecturer, publicist, and explorer Dr. Lyman Sperry, and other "preservationists," lobbied to designate the area a national park. They failed, but made two more attempts. On the third try, Louis Hill, who had always been in favor of the idea, joined the campaign and used his considerable influence as president of the Great Northern and son of the Empire Builder to urge Congress to pass the bill. Finally on May 11, 1910, President William Howard Taft signed the bill creating Glacier National Park.

ABOVE: *Ranger Frank Liebig on patrol in Glacier. Early 1900s.*
LIEBIG FAMILY ALBUM, PRIVATE COLLECTION

TOP: *Glacier's first Forest Ranger Station. Located at the head of Lake McDonald.*
LIEBIG FAMILY ALBUM, PRIVATE COLLECTION

America's Switzerland

Scenes of chalets and hotels on baggage labels.
COURTESY GLACIER NATIONAL PARK ARCHIVES

Louis envisioned this new and magnificent national park as America's Swiss Alps. The idea to compare the mountains and lakes of Glacier to the Alps was probably planted by Great Northern agent F. I. Whitney in 1894, when he wrote about Lake McDonald as "... set like a grand Kohinoor [a large diamond, one of the British Crown Jewels] in the midst of Alpine grandeur." Louis Hill's notion to portray Glacier as "America's Switzerland" was both romantic and practical. He genuinely loved the Rocky Mountain West and he wanted to lure wealthy tourists who traditionally vacationed in Europe to take the Great Northern to Glacier's alpine grandeur instead.

Louis Hill's vision of Glacier as America's Swiss Alps became his personal project. He, like his father, rolled up his sleeves and worked to make it happen. In 1912 he stepped down as president of the Great Northern and succeeded his father as chairman of the board. Between 1910 and 1913 he commissioned nine Swiss-style chalets around Glacier. They were constructed at Belton, St. Mary, Sun Point, Two-Medicine, Sperry, Granite Park, Cut Bank, and Gunsight Lake, and the grand Glacier Park Hotel was built at Midvale (now East Glacier).

Louis Hill personally selected the sites for the chalets and the hotels. In Ray Djuff and Chris Morrison's *Glacier's Historic Hotels & Chalets: View with a Room,* the authors offer that "The true genius of the accommodations was in Hill's site selection. Each location had a dramatically different scenic backdrop. Hill ensured the buildings were placed so guests could enjoy a view from every room. The use of the same rustic Swiss style for all the chalets ensured guests never lost the feeling of being somewhere special

and far away. It created a sense of place in a region of immense proportions."

While the chalets and lodge were being built, Hill contracted with Midvale businessman William J. Hilligoss to set up tent camps throughout the park, most of them near the chalets under construction or at sites where chalets would later be built.

The Great Northern also contracted to have tent camps constructed throughout the park in places that could be reached only on horseback or afoot, and offered guided tours throughout the park, with overnight stops at the camps. The tent camps lacked the comfortable accommodations easterners were used to, but they grew in popularity. The romance of the Wild West was in full swing. Dime novels had popularized outlaws, train robbers, cowboys, and Indians. Trail rides along the rivers and lake shores, over steep mountains and through eerie timbered forests, and living in tent and teepee camps on grass-covered meadows offered a safe taste of the Old West for an imaginative tourist. The flickering light of a campfire, sleeping on cots or in sleeping bags as their ancestors had, the nickering of horses grazing nearby, the hoot of an owl, a million stars shining in a black sky, the smell of coffee in the morning—they more than made up for a soft bed and elegantly served dinner. The adventure was long remembered after the tourists returned to the velvet luxuries of their homes. But many other tourists wanted the comforts of chalets, and Hill would provide both. In addition to the chalets he was building, he contracted for permanent tent camps at Red Eagle Lake, Goat Haunt, Cosley Lake, and Fifty Mountain.

At the time Hill was constructing chalets, there were very few trails or roads. Usable stage roads and horseback trails from chalet to chalet were required to accommodate the hoped-for tourists. The Department of Interior had allotted very little money to Glacier National Park so the Great Northern stepped in to finance roads and trails. In 1912, Hill brought in

Banff outfitters William and James Brewster to set up a saddle horse and stagecoach concession to operate between tent camps. On lakes and rivers where tour boats were needed, Hill contracted with Captain William Swanson to build the boats and run them for the railway. By 1917, the Great Northern would spend more than double the amount the government did to develop Glacier National Park and, by the late 1920s, had invested more than $2.3 million in the park's development.

There was little that Louis Hill and the Great Northern did not control or influence in the park. Permits for saddle horse and stagecoach operations and scenic tour boats were issued by the Department of Interior, later the National Park Service, but these permits were of little value if the Great Northern had not signed a private agreement allowing the concession to operate between its hotels and chalets. In 1914, Hill arranged with Walter White of the White Motor Company to provide autobus services in the park, and formed the Glacier Park Transportation Company to operate the little red buses. That same year, Hill, overwhelmed with his own success in bringing

business to Glacier, decided he could not continue to personally manage everything in the park as he had been—which was in minute, fussy detail, right down to selecting the flowers for the flower beds. He formed the Glacier Park Hotel Company, with its own managers and staff, and took an overseer role for himself. He then contracted for building the Many Glacier Hotel, which opened in 1915 on the site he had selected the year before, and the Prince of Wales Hotel in Waterton, which opened in 1927. He authorized the company to buy the Lewis Glacier Hotel on Lake McDonald that same year in anticipation of the completion of Going-to-the-Sun Road. By 1930, the Great Northern owned the facility and renamed it Lake McDonald Hotel.

Louis Hill resigned as chairman of the board of Great Northern in 1929. He had done the job he set out to do. He had built hotels, chalets, camps, riding and walking trails, and roads throughout the park. The visitor could enjoy the scenic wonders and Western adventure in a variety of comfort levels.

Louis Hill's resignation from the board of the Great Northern came concurrently with

BELOW LEFT: *Great Northern tour book, 1916.*
COURTESY K. ROSS TOOLE ARCHIVES, UNIVERSITY OF MONTANA, MISSOULA AND BURLINGTON-NORTHERN-SANTA FE RAILWAY

BELOW CENTER: *Glacier National Park teepee tent camp, 1916.*
GLACIER NATIONAL PARK WALKING TOURS BOOK, 1916; COURTESY BURLINGTON-NORTHERN-SANTA FE RAILWAY

BELOW RIGHT: *Two hearty hikers with their hotels on their backs tour Glacier National Park, 1916.*
GLACIER NATIONAL PARK WALKING TOURS BOOK, 1916; COURTESY BURLINGTON-NORTHERN-SANTA FE RAILWAY

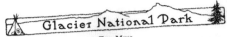

Glacier National Park

FOR MEN

Suit of old clothes, or khaki pants. Outing shirt. Sweater or wool jacket. Wool or cotton underwear of light weight. Heavy wool socks, and cotton socks to be worn next the foot. Hunting boots or stout laced shoes (either should be hobnailed). Canvas leggings (if shoes are worn). Felt hat or cap. Slicker or light rain coat. Light packsack for the carrying of luncheons and "miscellaneous."

FOR WOMEN

Short skirt, preferably divided. Middy blouse. In other respects same equipment as that specified for men.

Necessities for the Packsack

Adhesive Tape—to care for any feet blisters that develop. Talcum Powder—to prevent chafing of feet. Cold Cream—for possible sunburn. Collapsible drinking cup. Pocket flash lamp—enables you to "make camp" without worry if night happens to catch you short of your destination. Map of Glacier Park.

Some Items that Add to your Comfort and Enjoyment

Camera—a source of constant joy and in demand at every bend of the trail. Compass—not needed for following the trail but helpful in locating various topographical features of the Park—peaks, valleys and so on—in connection with map. Field Glasses—add much interest when on outlook places; particularly enjoyable for watching the Park's mountain goats and sheep. Colored Glasses—useful to those whose eyes are troubled by snowfields and glaciers.

Expressing of Baggage

Changes of clothing and all unessentials should be forwarded in grips or suit cases by the Park's automobile express service between the various hotels and chalet groups of the Park in accordance with the itinerary of the tourist afoot.

Costs

Save for minor incidental expenses the costs of tours of the foregoing character are the sums expended at the various hotels, chalets and tepee camps plus the fares covering such of the Park's travel services as the tourist chooses to make occasional use of.

All of the chalet groups of the Glacier Park Hotel Company on the American plan are operated on the uniform basis of $3.00 per day. Tariff for lodging, 75 cents; for breakfast, 75 cents; for luncheon, 75 cents; for evening dinner, 75 cents. Boxed luncheons, or other meals, for consumption "on the trail," 75

the inauguration of the Empire Builder train, its name honoring his father James J. Hill. These two events occurred on the brink of the Great Depression. Visitation to the park was declining and visitors by rail at an all-time low. The Great Northern's hotel business, even at its peak, had never been profitable for the railroad. The losses were written off as promoting rail travel and maintaining passenger traffic. By

1933, park visitor numbers had dropped so low that the St. Mary Chalet, the Prince of Wales Hotel, and the Cut Bank Chalet were not opened. The financial burden was becoming too great for a railroad already struggling to maintain its passenger service in the wake of growing automobile travel and the effects of the Depression. Faced with growing financial losses, Great Northern executives were rapidly losing interest in the hotel business and were concentrating their efforts in bringing new trains and better service to the line to compete with other railroads also struggling for shares of meager passenger revenues.

Meanwhile the programs of President Franklin D. Roosevelt to put the American people back to work gave life to the Civilian Conservation Corps and help to the National Park Service. The CCC was improving trails and roads, and the Park Service took a stronger role in directing operations of the Great Northern Hotel Company. The Park Service wanted the company to submit a five-year plan

ABOVE: *Guidance for the tourist seeing Glacier National Park afoot.*

GLACIER NATIONAL PARK WALKING TOURS BOOK, 1916; COURTESY BURLINGTON-NORTHERN-SANTA FE RAILWAY

RIGHT: *Advertising Great Northern's new Oriental Limited.*

COURTESY JOHN CHASE COLLECTION AND BURLINGTON, NORTHERN, SANTA FE RAILWAY

FAR RIGHT: *Great Northern Railway 1945 magazine ad.*

COURTESY ROBERT SMITH COLLECTION

for improvements in the park to meet visitor demands, which the company, for some reason, ignored. However, when the National Park Service requested the company build "auto cabin camps" throughout the park, the Great Northern reluctantly complied.

During the World War II years, passenger travel on the railroads grew, but few people took vacations. The Great Northern trains did not stop at Glacier. The park was essentially closed. Hotel employees were in the armed forces, and most of the hotels and chalets were closed. After the war, three of the chalets reached by horseback were not reopened and the Belton, Sperry, and Granite Park chalets were sold.

When Louis Hill died in 1948, the Great Northern executives began to aggressively work to rid the company of the hotel business in Glacier. In 1956, they negotiated with Donald T. Knutson, the owner of a Minneapolis construction company, to take over management of the hotels. The terms required that the Great Northern spend $3 million to renovate the buildings and, from 1957 to 1959, major changes were made to the hotels. Not all of them were good. Many of the distinct architectural features were destroyed to make way for Knutson's approach to hotel management. While Knutson was in charge, the Great Northern lost another $1.5 million. He was replaced by Don Hummel, who reversed the trend established by Knutson. In 1981, Hummel sold Glacier Park Inc. to Greyhound Food Management of Phoenix, Arizona.

See America First

When Louis Hill was busy developing the park, he had his Great Northern advertising agents busy producing railroad advertising to lure the tourists to Glacier. The creators of the impressive time tables, pamphlets, books, calendars, and railroad menu designs settled on three underlying themes: "See America First," "Glacier's Care-killing Scenery," and

"Living the Western Adventure in the home of the Blackfeet Indians."

The "See America First" slogan has been attributed to several tourism promoters including Louis Hill. It is not certain who actually coined the phrase, but it is generally believed to have been created during a meeting of railroad barons to discuss a campaign to lure wealthy tourists from the attractions of Europe. A "See America First" League was formed in 1906. American railroads spent millions every year to

Great Northern Time Table, 1914.

The Call of the Mountains

BY MARY ROBERTS RINEHART

Author of "Tenting To-night," "Through Glacier Park," "K," and Other Stories.

IF YOU are normal and philosophical, if you love your country, if you are willing to learn how little you count in the eternal scheme of things, go ride in the Rocky Mountains and save your soul.

There are no "Keep off the Grass" signs in Glacier National Park. It is the wildest part of America. If the Government had not preserved it, it would have preserved itself but you and I would not have seen it. It is perhaps the most unique of all our parks, as it is undoubtedly the most magnificent. Seen from an automobile or a horse, Glacier National Park is a good place to visit.

Here the Rocky Mountains run northwest and southeast, and in their glacier-carved basins are great spaces; cool shadowy depths in which lie blue lakes; mountain-sides threaded with white, where, from some hidden lake or glacier far above, the overflow falls a thousand feet or more, and over all the great silence of the Rockies. Here nerves that have been tightened for years slowly relax.

Here is the last home of a vanishing race — the Blackfeet Indians. Here is the last stand of the Rocky Mountain sheep and the Rocky Mountain goat; here are elk, deer, black and grizzly bears, and mountain lions. Here are trails that follow the old game trails along the mountain side; here are meadows of June roses, forget-me-not, larkspur, and Indian paint-brush growing beside glaciers, snowfields and trails of a beauty to make you gasp.

Here and there a trail leads through a snowfield; the hot sun seems to make no impression on these glacier-like patches. Flowers grow at their very borders, striped squirrels and whistling marmots run about, quite fearless, or sit up and watch the passing of horses and riders so close they can almost be touched.

The call of the mountains is a real call. Throw off the impediments of civilization. Go out to the West and ride the mountain trails. Throw out your chest and breathe — look across green valleys to wild peaks where mountain goats stand impassive on the edge of space. Then the mountains will get you. You will go back. The call is a real call.

I have traveled a great deal of Europe. The Alps have never held this lure for me. Perhaps it is because these mountains are my own — in my own country. Cities call — I have heard them. But there is no voice in all the world so insistent to me as the wordless call of these mountains. I shall go back. Those who go once always hope to go back. The lure of the great free spaces is in their blood.

Mary Roberts Rinehart

---

support the campaign. Louis Hill was a primary advocate, and the Great Northern added the slogan to virtually all of its time tables and brochures and to their symbol on the trains.

In John Muir's 1901 book, Our National Parks, he described Glacier as the "best care-killing scenery on the continent" and promised that a month-long visit "... would not be taken from the sum of your life. Instead of shortening it, it will indefinitely lengthen it and make you truly immortal." The theme of "Care-killing Scenery," with variations, would be used in Great Northern advertising for the next sixty years. It appealed to an ambitious, busy, stressed populace during the rise of American economic power at the turn of the twentieth century, and was equally appealing during the worrisome World War I years, the roaring, unruly decade of the '20s, the down and out '30s, and the jubilant post–World War II recovery.

The most successful and most remembered "Care-killing Scenery" theme joined the Indians' spiritual reverence for the earth with the sights and sounds of Glacier. Nearly all of the people who explored Glacier spoke of the

ABOVE: *Introduction by Mary Roberts Rinehart to Great Northern's* The Call of the Mountains *brochure.*

COURTESY K. ROSS TOOLE ARCHIVES, UNIVERSITY OF MONTANA, MISSOULA

RIGHT: *Cover of 1927 Great Northern brochure.*

COURTESY K. ROSS TOOLE ARCHIVES, UNIVERSITY OF MONTANA, MISSOULA

FAR RIGHT: *Great Northern Magazine advertisement. 1940s.*

COURTESY BURLINGTON-NORTHERN-SANTA FE RAILWAY

power of the mountains to calm the spirit and struggled to explain the aura of tranquility that seemed to radiate from the land. The Great Northern sponsored tours for well-known writers, encouraging them to write of their experiences in Glacier, and often published or subsidized their work.

The railroad's own advertising agents were both eloquent in describing the park and clever in coming up with descriptive phrases. But in a stroke of advertising genius, the Great Northern concluded the Indians had it right, when it created *The Call of the Mountains*. A young Indian was pictured—arms raised, facing the mountains, inviting the visitor to hear the call of the mountains—in the image most identified with Glacier's mountain scenery.

Mary Roberts Rinehart, popular novelist, playwright, and journalist, toured the mountains of Glacier in the early 1900s and was so taken with the experience she wrote of her adventures in *Through Glacier Park* published in 1916 and a sequel *Tenting To-Night* published two years later. Rinehart was often sought as a spokesperson. In 1925 Louis Hill commissioned her to write the introduction to a Great Northern brochure, *The Call of the Mountains*, promoting vacations in the park.

If there was one attraction America had that Europe did not, it was the Wild West. The world's image of the frontier landscape, peopled by the likes of mountain man Jim Bridger, scout Kit Carson, hard-riding, fast-shooting cowboys, and proud, fearless, sometimes savage Indians was born of fact, nurtured by myth and is distinctly and proudly American.

The images of the American West were helped along by the paintings of Edward Borein, Frederic Remington, and Charles Russell and romanticized in Owen Wister's bestselling novel *The Virginian*, Theodore Roosevelt's four-volume history *The Winning of the West*, and Zane Grey's novels *Wanderer of the Wasteland, West of the Pecos*, and *Riders of the Purple Sage*. Dime novels and pulp magazines such as

Western Story Magazine and *Wild West Weekly* produced "rip roaring" stories and serials of the Wild West. In 1883, Buffalo Bill Cody went on the road with his Wild West show,

A Blackfeet Indian Camp.

entertaining easterners with horsemanship, marksmanship, and frontier derring-do that symbolized the West and the American cowboy to everyone who saw the show. In 1887 he took his Wild West show to England and Europe. These symbols of the American West, however fanciful, were embraced by the world. The image of the lone cowboy on his horse standing guard over a herd of cattle became the symbol of America to the world.

The lore of America's Wild West of cowboys and Indians captivated easterners and rivaled the cultural legacies of Europe in attracting tourists. They would travel long distances to experience America's West, to ride over mountain trails, dine on fresh-caught trout from a remote stream, see a bear, sit around a campfire with a cowboy, and look into the haunting eyes of an American Indian.

The western railroads were fully aware of the attraction the Wild West of legend held for tourists around the world. Each line featured images of grand landscapes, cowboys, and Indians in its advertising throughout the years. Ironically, it had been the railroads that both gave birth to the "era of the cowboy"

Prepared by
REINCKE-ELLIS-YOUNGGREEN & FINN
520 No. Michigan Ave., Chicago

Great Northern Ad No. 2863
2¼"x80 lines
New Yorker, May 13, 1933
Time, May 22, 1933

I remember your face

● You're Two Guns White Calf, Chief of the Blackfeet tribe in Glacier Park. I'm anxious to see another of your pow-wows. I want to meet those ranger-naturalists again, and the good looking dude wranglers who guide, cook and lie like Baron Munchausen. I'll meet you this summer at

Glacier Park
on the route of the
Empire Builder
(If in doubt write A. J. Dickinson, P. T. M., 734 Great Northern Railway Bldg., St. Paul.)

GREAT NORTHERN

ABOVE: *Great Northern advertisement in 1930s brochure.*
COURTESY GLACIER NATIONAL PARK ARCHIVES AND BURLINGTON-NORTHERN-SANTA FE RAILWAY

TOP: *Blackfeet Indian camp.*
COURTESY GLACIER NATIONAL PARK ARCHIVES AND BURLINGTON-NORTHERN-SANTA FE RAILWAY

Western Adventure

You take a last tug at the latigo to tighten the cinch, swing easily into the saddle, the cowboy guide waves his hand forward, and, with the sound of creaking leather mingling with unhurried shouts, you set off on another exciting western adventure in Glacier National Park in the Montana Rockies. You start riding, instead of just cruising, when you become part of a scene like the one above. From that point on you are riding, hiking, motoring, boating, fishing, swimming your way through an endless panorama of thrilling experiences that will take your breath away with their memory in years to come.

"All West and over a Mile High," Glacier National Park is a magnificent part of America the Beautiful. Everything in it, from its craggy peaks, home of the surefooted mountain goat, to its trout filled crystal lakes and streams, is for your special vacation enjoyment. From the moment you step off the Great Northern's Oriental Limited at either the West or East entrance, you'll be champing to plunge into the deserts of activities that await your participation. In this folder we have tried to picture a few of

Glacier Park's wonders but no printed page can convey the thrill that will be yours when you discover for yourself each visit, each adventure that this tremendous mountain playground has to offer.

It is as simple to see and do things in Glacier Park. Motor coaches tour the highways, taking you right through the heart of the park via spectacular Going-to-the-Sun Highway. Well-marked trails pierce the vastness beyond the highway, making it possible for you to personally unlock the innermost secrets of this vast wonderland. Sight-seeing motor launches carry you up and down the larger lakes.

Facilities range from picturesque hotels to out-of-the-way chalets. Accommodations and meals are of the best. You can make one stay at the four hotels your "base of operations" as you fish, play golf, hike, ride, attend Blackfeet Indian ceremonials, stalk wild game with a camera, or just relax in the invigorating mountain atmosphere.

Now is the time to plan . . . this is the year to go . . . there's real Western Adventure waiting for you in Glacier National Park!

The Old West is still in the saddle at Glacier Park This summer let a trail-wise horse in Glacier Park lead you to the real West, carefree, vivid, ever youthful. Come climb a shining mountain, fish a lake of bottomless blue, hike over the crest of the Rockies—be active this vacation! For full details write Great Northern Vacations, St. Paul.
The New **EMPIRE BUILDER** The Luxurious **ORIENTAL LIMITED**

The Old West goes international in Glacier and Waterton Lakes Parks
This summer meet up with the Old West in this playground that straddles the Great Divide and the International Boundary—where scenery and sports are equally colorful! Go places in hiking boots, saddle, or bus and launch—do things you've never done before. Ride, fish, climb, camp out, explore—and enjoy true Canadian hospitality! Write Great Northern Vacations, St. Paul.
The New **EMPIRE BUILDER** The Luxurious **ORIENTAL LIMITED**

TOP: *Great Northern Railway brochure.*
COURTESY GLACIER NATIONAL PARK ARCHIVES
AND BURLINGTON-NORTHERN-SANTA FE RAILWAY

ABOVE AND RIGHT: *Great Northern Railway magazine ads.*
COURTESY JOHN CHASE COLLECTION AND
BURLINGTON, NORTHERN, SANTA FE RAILWAY

FAR RIGHT: *Great Northern Railway Walking Tours Book.*
COURTESY JOHN CHASE COLLECTION AND
BURLINGTON, NORTHERN, SANTA FE RAILWAY

and brought it to its close. In the 1840s, when the eastern network of rail lines were laid as far west as Missouri and Kansas and made ranching in the west and shipping to the East possible, that gave rise to the great cattle ranches and the western livestock business. The cowboy life was born. When the transcontinental railroads connected East to West and populated the space between, it brought an end to the fabled cowboy era of the American West. Rail lines crossed the prairies and mountains and, where they planted tracks, farms and towns rose and flourished and the civilized East came west. Open ranges, where Indians had once hunted buffalo, were homesteaded, farmed, and fenced off. Indians were pushed onto ever-shrinking reservations to make way for settlers. Trains reached all the country north and

south, east and west. Long cattle drives along the Shawnee, Chisholm, and Western trails to the railheads at Kansas City, Abilene, and Dodge City were no longer necessary and the great cattle drives ended. The era of the cowboy and the American West of legend slipped into history and became the "Old West."

The nation's romantic attachment to the Old West began in the 1880s and has never faded. In the early years of the twentieth century, the Great Northern set out to change the "direction of the west" in the hearts and minds of travelers. West was Northwest! The Old West or what remained of it still existed in Montana along Great Northern lines. Vast cattle ranches dotted the landscape. Where millions of buffalo once roamed, cattle still grazed under the watchful eye of Montana cowboys. The cowboy way was still evident in Montana towns, and Indians roamed the streets. Great Northern tracks ran through the Blackfeet Reservation then along Marias Pass bordering the country of the Blackfeet, Kutenai, and mountain man. The Old West, at least in part, could be seen from the windows of a Great Northern train and could be expe-

With the "MOUNTAINEERS" in GLACIER NATIONAL PARK

WALKING TOURS BOOK

LEFT: *Winold Reiss painting Buffalo Body.*

K. ROSS TOOLE ARCHIVES, UNIVERSITY OF MONTANA. COURTESY BURLINGTON-NORTHERN-SANTA FE RAILWAY

BELOW: *Hans Reiss demonstrating carving techniques at the Reiss Art School in Glacier National Park.*

K. ROSS TOOLE ARCHIVES, UNIVERSITY OF MONTANA. COURTESY BURLINGTON-NORTHERN-SANTA FE RAILWAY

rienced, however vaguely and unrealistically, on the mountain trails of Glacier.

The Great Northern's "Old West" advertising focused on the Blackfeet and referred to them as the "Glacier Park Indians." These once-great warriors of the plains resided on the reservation adjacent to Glacier National Park. Life on a reservation was an uneasy role for these proud, nomadic people, but they were forced to bend with the winds of time. The poverty that existed on nearly all of the reservations was somewhat lightened by the railroad's interest in the Blackfeet. Members of the tribe joined in the Great Northern's campaign to bring a piece of the romantic Old West to the traveler. Dressed in full regalia they met the trains at East Glacier, posed for photographs and films, put

Winold Reiss paintings of Blackfeet Indians.
COURTESY K. ROSS TOOLE ARCHIVES, UNIVERSITY OF MONTANA, MISSOULA AND BURLINGTON-NORTHERN-SANTA FE RAILWAY

their teepees on the grounds around the lodges, entertained tourists, worked for the saddle horse companies, and were a part of the Glacier scene. They received salaries from the Great Northern, were paid by artists and photographers for posing, and earned money from film companies when they appeared in motion pictures.

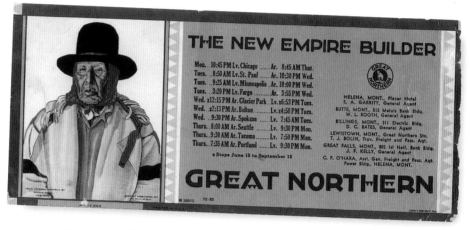

1932 Great Northern ink blotter. COURTESY BRUCE THISTED COLLECTION

Louis Hill, who actually had a great regard for the Blackfeet, was personally involved in the promotion of the Glacier Park Indians. He commissioned artists Kathryn Leighton, Julius Seyler, and W. Langdon Kihn to paint the Blackfeet. But the artist to become most identified with the Blackfeet of Glacier National Park was Winold Reiss.

German-born Reiss immigrated to this country in 1913. He had studied art at the Munich Academy and arrived with a romantic image of the American West. His goal was to seriously study the American Indian. He decided on the Blackfeet tribe and, in 1919, took a Great Northern passenger train to Browning, Montana, the headquarters of the Blackfeet

Nation. In Scott J. Tanner's biography of Winold Reiss written for the Great Northern Railway Historical Society, Tanner quotes a 1935 newspaper interview with Reiss about his first day at the reservation:

"I had read books about how you must always approach an Indian with ceremony, but I just ran down and rushed up to the biggest, finest looking one, and slapped him on the back, and began telling him how I had come all the way to see my red brothers and paint them."

The Indian was the six-foot-tall former warrior Angry Bull. Angry Bull, like many of the elders, did not speak English or at best understood very little. He had no idea what the exuberant Reiss was saying. Fortunately, someone who did understand English overheard the exchange and stepped up to interpret. When Angry Bull realized he was being asked to pose for a painting he demanded $10 an hour, the same fee as the Blackfeet were receiving for their appearances in motion pictures being filmed in the park. After some haggling, Angry Bull agreed to pose for 50 cents an hour and cigarettes.

During Reiss's three-week visit to Montana, he worked intensely, completing thirty-five portraits of the Blackfeet and a self-portrait. While doing so, Reiss's diligent work and dignified portraits earned the respect of the Blackfeet, and they honored him with a ceremony at which they bestowed on him the

Indian name of *Ksistakpoka*—Beaver Child.

The portraits were displayed at the E. F. Hanfstaengl Gallery in New York and purchased by Dr. Philip Cole, and are now part of the Bradford Brinton Memorial Museum in Big Horn, Wyoming.

In 1923, Winold's brother Hans immigrated to America. Hans had chronic hay fever and, in the spring of 1925 on the advice of his brother, sought relief in Montana's mountain air. Hans, who had experience as a mountain climbing guide in Norway and Lapland, was hired as a climbing guide in the Grinnell Glacier area by the Park Saddle Horse Company. His climbing experience and European accent and style of dress were a perfect fit for this "Swiss Alps of America." A press release described him as "the first European guide ever engaged by the park people." That summer, Hans served as the climbing guide for Louis Hill. There is no record that Hans discussed his brother's work with the Blackfeet with Hill at the time. But several months later—in January 1926—Hans wrote to Hill and included some photos of Winold's Blackfeet portraits. Louis Hill replied within two weeks indicating his interest in having Winold come to the park to do more Blackfeet portraits. Hill sent a memo to the Great Northern's General Advertising Agent, W. R. Mills, asking him to make arrangements for Reiss to come west and stating that "I think this man is one of the best prospects we have had in the way of artists painting Indian pictures, which are our strongest feature, and it takes a good artist to make them."

Winold had already accepted another commission that kept him occupied for the summer, but the following year, the railroad made another and better offer. In 1927, Winold Reiss, accompanied by his son Tjark, returned to the home of the Blackfeet.

That summer Reiss completed fifty-one portraits. In addition to painting the Pikuni Blackfeet who inhabited the Blackfeet Reservation adjacent to Glacier, Reiss went to Canada to paint the Blood Indians of the Blackfoot Confederation. Louis Hill was opening the Great Northern's Prince of Wales Hotel that July and was eager to include the Canadian Indians in his advertising. Reiss came to Glacier in 1928 to paint another twenty-nine portraits for the railway. In 1934 Reiss once again returned to the park, this time to establish the Winold Reiss Summer Art School under the auspices of New York University and the reluctant sponsorship of

Cover of book of Winold Reiss paintings of the Blackfeet Indians.
COURTESY K. ROSS TOOLE ARCHIVES, UNIVERSITY OF MONTANA, MISSOULA AND BURLINGTON-NORTHERN-SANTA FE RAILWAY

BLACKFEET INDIANS
AN UNUSUAL BOOK

SHOT ON BOTH SIDES—CHIEF OF THE BLOOD INDIANS

the Great Northern. In 1943, a new contract was made for additional Blackfeet portraits for Great Northern calendars. That summer Reiss completed sixty-six new portraits. Reiss' last trip to Glacier National Park was in 1948.

The Winold Reiss paintings were used on Great Northern calendars for over thirty years. The railway also used them on dining car and hotel menus, ink blotters, playing cards, post cards, and brochures on Glacier National Park.

During Scott Tanner's research for his *A Biography of Winold Reiss: The Man Who Created the Great Northern Railway's Blackfeet Indian Portraits,* he was fortunate to visit Tjark Reiss in New York. Tjark provided Scott with an enlightened view of Winold Reiss. He wrote: "Reiss's grandest dream went unfulfilled. He hoped throughout much of his life, to complete a series of portraits of Native Americans across the United States for what he dubbed the *Monument to the American Indian.*" Reiss intended to assemble a collection of over 300 portraits to preserve the legacy of the older Indians who were the last of their people to have known life before the reservation. Unfortunately he was unable to get the commercial or philanthropic backing to realize his dream.

Winold Reiss died in 1953 following a series of strokes. In July 1954, the Blackfeet tribe held a ceremony at Red Blanket Hill to honor him. George Bullchild led the group of mourners in traditional Blackfeet prayers and songs, then they scattered Reiss's ashes to the wind.

While the basic themes of "See America First," "Care-killing Scenery," and the west-

ern adventure would continue through the years, the advertising would wisely reflect the times.

ROCKY

The most enduring, nationally known symbol of the Great Northern Railway is a mountain goat standing on a rock. This symbol—affectionately nicknamed Rocky—has taken many forms over the years, from stately monarch of the mountains to talking, suitcase-carrying caricature. He identifies Great Northern trains and is the symbol of Glacier National Park.

Since the first locomotive was introduced in America in 1829 the machine has been known as the "iron horse"—a monster steed, breathing fire and belching smoke, thundering over the prairies

Glacier National Park hotels and chalets open for the 1946 summer season after a long closure during World War II.

COURTESY MR. LINDSAY KORST, GREAT NORTHERN RAILWAY HISTORICAL SOCIETY, WEBMASTER

"**Welcome Back to Glacier Park!**"

"That grin I'm wearing has been a long, long time busting through my whiskers, but blow my horns if I haven't something to grin about!

"They're opening the hotels and chalets in Glacier National Park this summer for folks who've craved for an eyeful of the most eye-filling country in the U.S.A. Come out this summer for a real Western vacation."

June 15 is the most important date on America's first postwar vacation calendar. It's the opening day of the 1946 summer vacation season in Glacier National Park

on the route of Great Northern's transcontinental Empire Builder.

Up in northwestern Montana, where the American and Canadian Rockies shake hands, Glorious Glacier is the place for the most refreshing vacation of your life—the one you've been wanting and needing.

A letter or postcard to A. J. Dickinson, Passenger Traffic Manager, Great Northern Railway, St. Paul 1, Minnesota, will bring you complete descriptive material on summer vacation or stop-off tours in Glacier National Park.

GREAT NORTHERN RAILWAY
BETWEEN GREAT LAKES AND PACIFIC

This booklet illustrates and describes each car of the NEW Empire Builder. Check the accommodations you would like and turn to the pages that describe them. Following the

and plains, galloping up the distances with the "wings of the wind." When the Great Northern locomotives crossed the Rocky Mountains, the beast took on a different image and a different name—"the iron goat." The heavy mountain locomotives that scaled the steep slopes and rugged terrains of the Rockies were likened to the sure-footed monarch of the high mountains—the mountain goat—and trainmen began calling their locomotives iron goats. Early switcher engines were known as yard goats, but not for the same respectful reason. Yard goats moved things around rail yards, much like a domestic goat trained to pull carts. The majestic mountain goat ruled the high mountains, traversing them with ease. The owner of the Great Northern—that heavy-chested, white-bearded, one-eyed rumbling force James J. Hill—was occasionally called "the iron goat" by his contemporaries for his iron-thick hide and stubborn purposeful will.

However, it was not for these reasons that, in 1921, Louis Hill adopted the Glacier mountain goat as the symbol of the Great Northern Railway. He chose the mountain goat as a symbolic link between the railroad and Glacier National Park.

The logo changed forms and colors over the years beginning with the "facing goat logo" in 1921, and then changed to a side profile in 1936. The side profile was used until 1967 when the Great Northern adopted the "Big Sky Blue" theme and a modern stylized goat.

ABOVE: *Rocky coaster.*
COURTESY JOHN CHASE COLLECTION AND BURLINGTON, NORTHERN, SANTA FE RAILWAY

RIGHT: *Great Northern Railway logos.*
COURTESY MR. LINDSAY KORST, GREAT NORTHERN RAILWAY HISTORICAL SOCIETY, WEBMASTER

BELOW: *Great Northern Railway streamliner brochure.*
COURTESY JOHN CHASE COLLECTION AND BURLINGTON, NORTHERN, SANTA FE RAILWAY

 1895

 1914

 1921

 1922

to

 1935

 1936

 1967

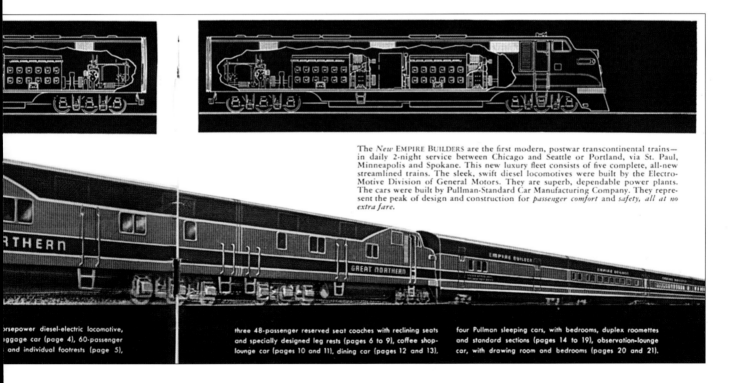

The *New* EMPIRE BUILDERS are the first modern, postwar transcontinental trains—in daily 2-night service between Chicago and Seattle or Portland, via St. Paul, Minneapolis and Spokane. This new luxury fleet consists of five complete, all-new streamlined trains. The sleek, swift diesel locomotives were built by the Electro-Motive Division of General Motors. They are superb, dependable power plants. The cars were built by Pullman-Standard Car Manufacturing Company. They represent the peak of design and construction for *passenger comfort* and *safety*, all at no extra fare.

rsepower diesel-electric locomotive, ggage car (page 4), 60-passenger and individual footrests (page 5),

three 48-passenger reserved seat coaches with reclining seats and specially designed leg rests (pages 6 to 9), coffee shop-lounge car (pages 10 and 11), dining car (pages 12 and 13),

four Pullman sleeping cars, with bedrooms, duplex roomettes and standard sections (pages 14 to 19), observation-lounge car, with drawing room and bedrooms (pages 20 and 21).

Great Northern 1920s advertising art.

CHAPTER 7

Hear that Lonesome Whistle Blow

By the time the Great Northern transcontinental railroad was completed in 1893, the golden age of railroads that had begun three decades earlier was reaching its peak. Railroads had become the chief form of transportation, and Henry Ford's first car was just being built. While Ford was tinkering with his internal combustion engine and the Hills were driving the last spike of their transcontinental railroad, the financial depression of 1893 hit. The Great Northern's network of rails connecting to the main line was already carrying enough traffic to pay for itself, and the Great Northern not only survived the financial crisis, but also added to its empire.

When prosperity returned in 1897, the glory days of railroad passenger trains were born. The rapidly growing middle class as well as the wealthy could afford to travel, and vigorous competition between the railroads for passenger revenue brought faster trains, grandly built stations, and luxurious service.

The heavy wooden cars designed for long-distance trains were replaced by impressive cars in the Victorian style. They were made of hardwoods, varnished to glistening, and decorated with gold striping. The Great Northern coaches featured arched windows embellished with leaded glass. The interiors were elegant rooms with tall arch-style ceilings, heavy draperies, and tapestry-covered upholstery. The parlor car and diners were lush lounges where passengers relaxed, talked, played cards, and looked out at the passing scenery. Even more prestigiously lush were the smoking cars, also known as

club cars, which were the sole province of men. There they could enjoy a glass of liquor, smoke a cigar, and discuss their exploits in business, hunting, and women. Nothing was finer than dinner in the diner where gourmet meals, usually at high prices, were served in the aristocratic manner of the East's finest restaurants. It was no simple task to run the dining car. The Great Northern steward had to know passenger traffic and predict how seasons affected appetites and bring

The Oriental Limited in the heart of the Rockies.
COURTESY MONTANA HISTORICAL SOCIETY

enough food aboard to last the trip. Some items, such as the Rocky Mountain trout, were supplied fresh along the way. The Great Northern was known for its chicken pies, biscuits, and dinner rolls, which were prepared and baked in the train kitchen on charcoal-burning stoves. Chefs, cooks, waiters, and stewards were periodically sent to schools to learn the latest innovations in food preparation and meal service.

In addition to the brochures and timetables inviting passengers to journey on their trains, the railroad advertising agents added another dimension to their publicity: naming the trains. It had started in the 1880s but did not become widespread until the 1900s. The first Great Northern transcontinental revenue-producing passenger train was not named. It was known simply as Number 3 & 4, advertised as "Solid Trains to the Northwest," and had a running time from St. Paul to Seattle of seventy-five hours. The Great Northern inaugurated its transcontinental passenger service with E-7 ten-wheeler locomotives, but the reliable standard of the railroads, the 4-4-0s continued to handle much of the journey. In addition to the baggage/express car, day coach, diner and buffet car, and Barney & Smith sleepers that had twelve sections, three compartments, a smoking room, a state room, and an open vestibule, Great Northern offered wealthy passengers new, more luxurious coaches finished in polished oak, with ten sections and two staterooms. These were given names of places along the line—Marias, Flathead, Spokane, Columbia, Wenatchee, and Peshastin. The spartan "free colonist cars"

Locomotive Classifications

Locomotives are classified by wheel arrangements—lead wheels, driver wheels, and under-the-cab wheels. For example a 4-4-0 has four wheels on its lead truck, four drivers, and no wheels under the cab.

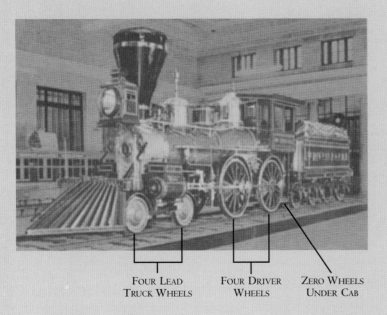

FOUR LEAD TRUCK WHEELS   FOUR DRIVER WHEELS   ZERO WHEELS UNDER CAB

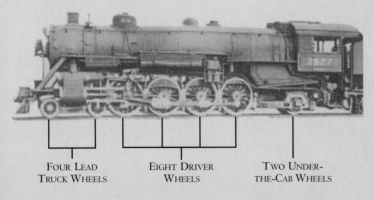

FOUR LEAD TRUCK WHEELS   EIGHT DRIVER WHEELS   TWO UNDER-THE-CAB WHEELS

COURTESY MR. LINDSAY KORST, GREAT NORTHERN RAILWAY HISTORICAL SOCIETY, WEBMASTER

Great Northern advertising art.

COURTESY JOHN CHASE COLLECTION AND BURLINGTON, NORTHERN, SANTA FE RAILWAY

were converted to "tourist cars" for the not so well heeled. By 1895, the Great Northern cut its running time to sixty-nine hours, added an observation and buffet-library car, featured "magnificent dining cars," and decided that naming trains was a good idea. The train was christened The Limited. In the train world Limited meant limited stops and faster travel, and also became synonymous with luxury trains.

In 1899, the Great Northern again cut its running time to an amazing, for its time, 64.15 hours. This fast schedule beat the Northern Pacific's, and the U.S. Post Office gave the Pacific Fast Mail contract to Great Northern. Heavier E-3 ten-wheelers were purchased to make the faster run, and sixty-five-foot mail cars were delivered to handle the mail. This train was named The Great Northern Flyer to emphasis its speed. The Flyer was renumbered from 3 & 4 to 1 & 2 in 1903, and featured an elegantly appointed Victorian style buffet-library-observation car.

In 1905 the Great Northern's transcontinental train underwent another name change. For a short time it was known as The Great Northern Limited that featured "palatial sleeping cars." Then in December the name was changed to the Oriental Limited to publicize the Great Northern's connection to the Far East.

In 1900, James J. Hill had put into motion the start of his youthful dream of going to the Orient. A genius in marketing, he had studied the reports of China, Japan, and India and calculated that "if a single province of China should consume an ounce a day of our flour, they would need 50,000,000 bushels of wheat per annum, or twice the Western surplus." It would create a great new market for western wheat and the Hill lines. He then convinced industrialists in China, Japan, and India to buy Southern raw cotton, American rails, New England cotton goods, Minnesota flour, and Colorado metals, and formed the Great Northern Steamship Company to ship these goods to the Far East. Hill issued contracts for two ships, the *Minnesota* and the *Dakota*. In

Magazine ad.
COURTESY JOHN CHASE COLLECTION AND BURLINGTON, NORTHERN, SANTA FE RAILWAY

Free Colonist / Zulu Car

The transcontinental immigrant sleeping cars were sparely furnished, usually with boxlike wooden cubicles built along each side of the car. Wooden straight-backed seats faced each other so that boards could be placed across them to form beds. Above the double seats, a pull-down wooden bunk was attached to the wall by a chain. Immigrants had to furnish their own bedding. At one end was a single "saloon" (restroom) and at the other end a sink with a water tank and a cooking stove so that the immigrants could prepare their meals on long journeys. In the West, these "colonist cars" were known as "Zulu cars."

Illustration of the interior of the St. Paul, Minneapolis & Manitoba Railroad "colonist sleeper" published in the 1889 Railroad Gazette.
PRIVATE COLLECTION

BOTTOM: *The steamships* Dakota *and* Minnesota *at the Great Northern docks in Seattle. 1917.*
COURTESY JOHN CHASE COLLECTION, GREAT FALLS, MT

BELOW: *The steamship* Minnesota.
COURTESY JOHN CHASE COLLECTION, GREAT FALLS, MT

1905, the *Minnesota* and the *Dakota* began sailing between Seattle and Yokohama and Hong Kong. Hill was once again in the steamship business. In 1914, the Great Northern Pacific Steamship Company was formed by the Great Northern and Hill's Northern Pacific Railroad. The company launched two more ships, the *Great Northern* and the *Northern Pacific*. Known as the Twin Palaces of the Pacific, these provided fast passenger service from the railhead at Portland, Oregon, to San Francisco, California, and were a steady annoyance to the Southern Pacific. The steamers offered round trips, with meals and berth, for $32 from Portland to San Francisco and the trip took about thirty hours

one way. The Southern Pacific's fastest train from Portland to San Francisco—the extra-fare Shasta Limited—took only three hours less time and cost more. Hill's ships carried freight and passengers along the coast and offered cruises to Hawaii. Great Northern and Northern Pacific Railway timetables included the steamship schedules.

The Oriental Limited train became the flagship of the Great Northern Railway. Its running time was sixty hours westbound and sixty-four hours eastbound between Puget Sound and St. Paul. In 1906 the Oriental Limited was powered by the Great Northern's first 4-4-2 locomotives, with 4-6-2s to take the train across the Rockies and the Cascades. The train consisted of a baggage-mail-express car, coaches, family tourist car, a smoker, dining car, sleepers, and compartment observation car. In 1909, when the Seattle World's Fair took place, the Oriental Limited was re-equipped to handle the millions of visitors expected to attend the event. The train was powered by H-4 Pacific locomotives. The *consist* (railroad term for train equipment) remained essentially the same but the gas lamps were replaced by electrically lighted lamps, and restrooms were replaced by improved models. In 1914, the class P-1 Mountain type locomotives used to cross Marias Pass and the Cascades were added. By 1909, the Oriental Limited's route was extended east to Chicago over the rails of the Chicago, Burlington & Quincy Railroad, which Hill controlled after a stock buy-out in 1901.

In 1903, traffic in both directions on the Great Northern lines warranted a second transcontinental train. This service took the Numbers 3 & 4, and the west-bound train was named The Puget Sound Express, with the eastbound version the Eastern Express. In 1906, the train was renamed The Fast Mail and in 1910 the Oregonian to recognize the new through-route to Portland. Just prior to the opening of the four-story, 162-room Many Glacier Hotel in 1915, the Oregonian was

1055—Steamship Minnesota. Seattle Oriental Liner. Length 630 Feet, Carrying Capacity 23,000 Long Tons, Equal to 100 Trains of 25 Cars Each.

Steamers DAKOTA and MINNESOTA at the Great Northern Docks, Length each 670 feet and Tonnage Each 30 000. The Largest steamers in the World. Also the Japanese Steamer IYO Maru, length 460 feet Tonnage 7000 Seattle Wash.

renamed the Glacier Park Limited. It had a
running time from St. Paul to Seattle of sixty
hours. The line had long advertised "the scenes
along the line" from the window of a Great
Northern train. To make its premier tourist
attraction—Glacier National Park—even more
enjoyable for its passengers, it ran compartment
observation cars year-round, and open observation cars along the southern border of Glacier
and through the Cascades in summer.

The Glacier Park Limited was a popular
tourist train until World War I, when the
United States Railway Administration took
over operations of the nation's railroads. The
USRA cut back unnecessary civilian travel and
required that the long-haul limiteds also handle
local traffic. As a result the Glacier Park
Limited did not operate again west of Havre,
Montana, until after the war. In 1929, when
the Empire Builder went into service as the
premier Great Northern train, the Glacier Park
Limited was replaced by the old flagship of

INSET: *Two 1948 Oriental Limiteds
stopped at Glacier Park Station.*
COURTESY COLLECTION OF JOHN CHASE,
GREAT FALLS, MT

RIGHT: *Westbound Oriental Limited
powered by a P-2 locomotive stops at
Glacier Park Station in 1948.*
PHOTOGRAPHER: JOHN CHASE WITH A KODAK
BABY BROWNIE CAMERA. COURTESY COLLEC-
TION OF JOHN CHASE, GREAT FALLS, MT

Oriental
Limited
A "Woman's
Train"

manicurist—a maid, valet,
hairdresser, or barber
ready to serve you. Surely
you never lack for accustomed
personal service when you travel
on the Oriental Limited.

A. J. DICKINSON
Passenger Traffic Manager
St. Paul, Minn.

GREAT NORTHERN

A Dependable Railway

Sixty Miles of Glacier National Park from Car Window

RIGHT: *Promoting the
Oriental Limited as
a "Woman's Train."*
COURTESY MINNESOTA
HISTORICAL SOCIETY

BELOW: *Scenes of interiors
of Great Northern trains
showing the comforts they
provide. 1920s Great
Northern brochure.*
COURTESY K. ROSS TOOLE
ARCHIVES, UNIVERSITY OF
MONTANA, MISSOULA AND
BURLINGTON-NORTHERN-
SANTA FE RAILWAY

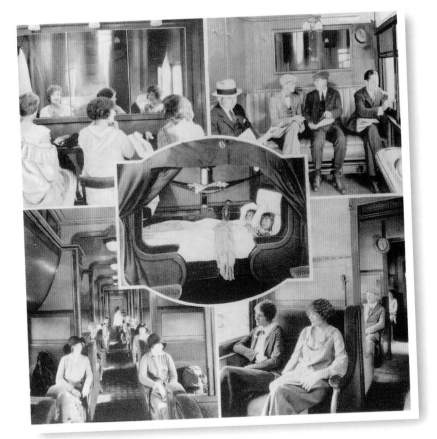

the Great Northern the Oriental Limited.

After the war, the government returned
the railroads to their owners under the
Transportation Act of 1920. The act also added
stringent new regulations for the railroad industry. This came at the same time that the use of
automobiles, buses, and trucks to haul passengers and freight was steadily climbing. These
new forms of transportation took huge bites
out of railroad revenues and threatened to sink
the industry altogether. Unlike some other railroads, the financially strong Great Northern
made it through these unsettling times without
much strain. But luring passengers back to the
railroads and hanging onto its own share of the
market took on primal importance. The Great
Northern upgraded luxury passenger service to a
new high. On June 1, 1924, the Great Northern
inaugurated a stunning new Oriental Limited. It
featured quiet, easy-riding passenger cars and,
for the first time, Pullman sleepers. Prior to
1922, the Great Northern operated its own dining and sleeping cars, but in 1922 Pullman took
over the sleeping-car operations and furnished a
luxurious Oriental Limited considered the
"Aristocrat of the Rails." Added features for the
busy traveler were telegraphic news bulletins and
stock market reports. The Oriental Limited was
also promoted as a "Woman's Train" and featured a woman's smoking lounge in the observation car and beauty parlor service. The Oriental
Limited remained the flagship of the Great
Northern until 1929 when it took second place
to the Empire Builder. The Oriental Limited
was discontinued in 1931 as passenger travel
decreased during the Depression.

Visits to Glacier had steadily increased since
the war and, by 1929, the park was enjoying a
booming tourist business. Great Northern passengers could get off the train at Midvale (East
Glacier), photograph the Blackfeet who met the
train, then take a Great Northern motorized
twelve-passenger bus to the Many Glacier Hotel
over the newly built, Great Northern–spon-

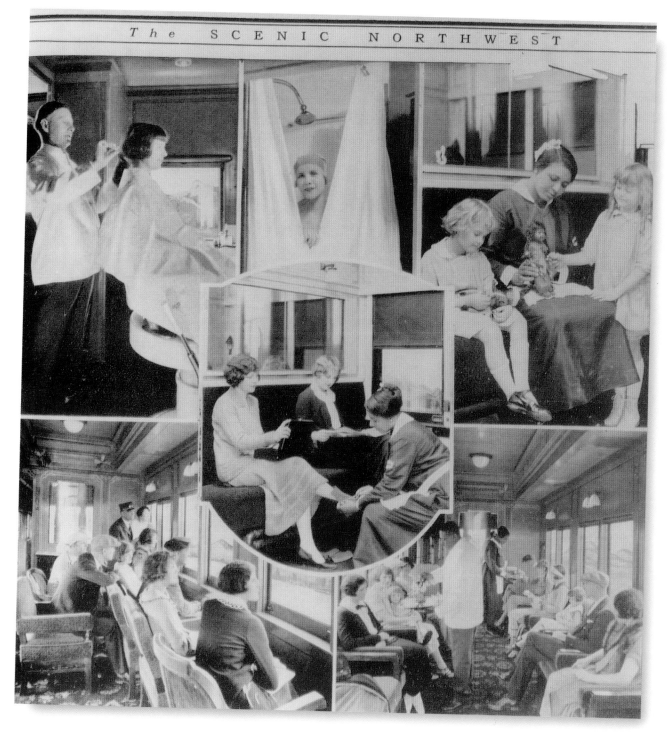

The SCENIC NORTHWEST

sored, motor-car road. Great Northern and National Park Service improvements were being made throughout the park, with Great Northern leading the effort and spending the most.

At the same time the Great Northern hotels, chalets, and camp investments in Glacier were experiencing exciting new interest, travel to the park by train was decreasing. In the 1920s roughly two-thirds of the national

parks were being visited by private automobile. As early as 1915, a road for motor cars across the mountains in Glacier National Park was being considered. Louis Hill wanted the road built along the Swiftcurrent Pass route to his Many Glacier Hotel. Other proposals were made by Lyman Sperry, as well as R. B. Marshall of the U.S. Geological Survey. Government surveys found that over Logan

Scenes of interiors of Great Northern trains. 1920s Great Northern brochure.

COURTESY K. ROSS TOOLE ARCHIVES, UNIVERSITY OF MONTANA, MISSOULA AND BURLINGTON-NORTHERN-SANTA FE RAILWAY

ABOVE: *Scenes of interiors of Great Northern trains. 1920s Great Northern brochure.*
COURTESY K. ROSS TOOLE ARCHIVES, UNIVERSITY OF MONTANA, MISSOULA AND BURLINGTON-NORTHERN-SANTA FE RAILWAY

BELOW: *Great Northern book advertising the Empire Builder.*
GLACIER NATIONAL PARK ARCHIVES AND BURLINGTON-NORTHERN-SANTA FE

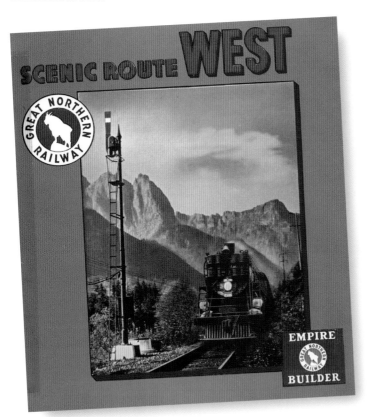

Pass from popular Lake McDonald to St. Mary's was the most practical route, and construction of Going-to-the-Sun Road began in the 1920s. The park's other automobile road was U.S. Highway 2 along the southern border and within sight of the Great Northern tracks. Also under construction in the 1920s, U.S. Highway 2 would be completed in 1930.

Besides having a vested interest in encouraging travel by train to Glacier National Park, the Great Northern also needed to stay ahead of the competition in luring passengers back to the transcontinental railroads. In 1929, the Great Northern upped the ante in luxury trains again when it introduced the Empire Builder, honoring James J. Hill, on June 10. By now, the Cascade Tunnel in Washington had been completed, shortening the running time from Chicago to Seattle by ten hours to just over sixty-one hours. This fast, premier luxury train was powered by Mountain P-2s until the oil-burning Northern locomotives came in later. It included the latest Pullman roller-bearing passenger cars, and such amenities as a men's bath and barbershop, and tubs and showers for women. It consisted of the baggage car, dormitory/coach/smoking-lounge car, two refurbished Barney and Smith coaches, three tourist sleeping cars, the dining car, three first-class sleeping cars and the buffet/lounge/solarium/observation car. Cheerful interiors replaced the sedate décor of the past. The Empire Builder would take many forms in the decades to come—new locomotives, new luxury cars, new paint schemes—and it would become the most popular train ever.

The Empire Builder was debuted just four months before the stock market crashed and the beginning of the world-wide crisis and the Great Depression of the 1930s. During the troubled times of the '30s, railroads had to reduce operating costs or fall into receivership. They diminished station and building upkeep, reduced or stopped train service on many of their short lines, and closed many depots. Even the financially strong Great Northern was forced to reduce its annual common stock dividends for the first time since 1892. Visits to Glacier dropped to the lowest level since it became a park. The Great Northern cut fares and accelerated promotional efforts, but that did little to increase park visitation. In 1933, the Glacier Park Hotel Company closed the Cut Bank and St. Mary chalets and the Prince of Wales Hotel.

Seeking to lure passengers back to their long-haul trains, all the railroads began improving their equipment, despite the bad times and their financial losses. In the 1930s, in the midst of the Great Depression, the era of the streamliner was born when the Union Pacific unveiled its City of Salina diesel locomotive and the Chicago, Burlington & Quincy its Zephyr. The Great Northern took a more conservative approach in adapting to diesels on its long-haul trains. They had just recently inaugurated the luxury Empire Builder and were not ready to make the change to streamliners despite the competition. However, when the Union Pacific announced it would air-condition its luxury train to increase passenger comfort, it forced the Great Northern to so the same. In 1935, the Empire Builder became the first completely air-conditioned transcontinental train in the Northwest. These added comforts and the usually successful railroad advertising blitz of the period made little impact during those troubled times, and passenger revenues continued to plummet.

When the Depression ended and the nation went to war in the 1940s, railroad freight and passenger service rose dramatically. Gasoline and tire rationing restricted automobile use, buses could not handle the enormous passenger loads and, with the nation recovering from the Depression with high wages in the shipyards and aircraft factories, once again railroads operated at a profit. The passenger load due to troop travel alone was staggering. In 1943, the

RIGHT: *1953 Great Northern magazine ad.*
COURTESY COLLECTION OF ROBERT SMITH

For a great vacation
Glacier Park
and the Pacific Northwest

Vacation *all the way*...Go Streamlined
WESTERN STAR

Imagine a playground rimmed by the Montana Rockies . . . laced with trout streams like Swiftcurrent, above . . . dotted with lakes . . . where mountain hotels await you. Vacation in Glacier National Park, gateway to the Pacific Northwest. Go carefree, be car-free!

For western travel and vacation information on ( ) Glacier Park, ( ) Pacific Northwest, ( ) California, write P. G. Holmes, Great Northern Ry., Dept. S-33, St. Paul 1, Minn.

Great Northern passenger and freight offices in all principal cities.

SEE AMERICA FIRST

ABOVE: *The Empire Builder crossing Midvale Creek Bridge at Glacier National Park in December 1970.*
COURTESY COLLECTION OF JOHN CHASE, GREAT FALLS, MT

TOP: *Empire Builder sporting the Big Sky Blue paint scheme stops at Glacier Park Station.*
COURTESY COLLECTION OF JOHN CHASE, GREAT FALLS, MT

were closed during the Depression remained closed, and others were idle. The Great Northern, along with the other railroads, "went to war." It did not promote travel to Glacier on its Empire Builder. The Great Northern Railway was busy transporting freight as a military supply line and the Empire Builder had taken on a new image—that of the patriot hauling servicemen to fight the war in the Pacific.

After the war, train travel returned to its steady decline. During the latter 1940s and throughout the 1950s, the nation's railroads struggled to hold on to a share of the passenger travel market. New federally funded highways made travel by automobile easier. Glacier National Park visits climbed to 300,000 in 1946 and soared to 500,000 by 1951. Only 2 percent of the visitors arrived by train. Airline passenger service was on the rise, offering faster travel times and previously unimagined in-flight luxury. During the fifteen years following the war, the railroads spent millions on equipment and services to stimulate passenger traffic, introducing new streamliners, better air-conditioning, new décor, more comforts, domed coaches and lounge cars, and lower rates. Advertising reached new heights. The Great Northern returned to its role of encouraging tourists to Glacier National Park, but the advertising no longer focused on the park as a destination. It emphasized getting there by train with such slogans as "Go Great ... Go Great Northern."

For the next decade and a half, the Great Northern introduced a series of new Empire Builders, beginning in 1947 when they entered the streamliner era. On February 7, the Great Northern inaugurated its Glacier Park green and orange streamliner. This new Empire Builder was the first of the postwar-built streamliners. It was powered with two-unit E-7 road passenger diesel-electric locomotives, offered forty-five-hour service between Chicago and the Pacific Northwest, and introduced innovations in passenger train service: duplex roomettes, reclining coach seats, assigned reserved coach seats, coffee

railroads, struggling to handle the necessary wartime passenger traffic, eliminated resort trains and used the equipment for moving troops, freight, and mail. Vacation travel virtually came to a halt. Visitor numbers in Glacier National Park plunged from 180,000 in 1941 to 23,000 in 1943. By 1943, the Empire Builder was whistling through East Glacier and West Glacier without stopping because of wartime troop and shipping schedules. Bus service inside the park was terminated. Chalets that

shop, dining-car reservations, ice-water drinking fountains in the coaches and sleeping cars, public-address system, and a traveling passenger representative as part of the train crew.

In 1950, when the Korean War began, the railroads once again saw an increase in passenger traffic, primarily for armed forces personnel. The increased traffic, however temporary, created a demand for additional sleeping cars to be added to the Empire Builder. Instead of simply ordering additional sleepers the Great Northern put all-new cars into service, essentially re-equipping the train. When the new train began operating in 1951 it was advertised as the all-new Mid-Century Empire Builder. The Mid-Century brought an even greater level of luxury to its Empire Builder and featured the western frontier in its interior motif. Popularity of the Old West was once again on the rise and the Great Northern took full advantage of the nation's love affair with the scenes of the West. The new *consist* included the G Bar N Ranch Lounge Car, which was decorated with replicas of cattle brands, leather furnishings, and murals of cattle drives. The Ranch Car became the most popular car of the Empire Builder. In contrast to the lounge's bold western motif, the dining car was decorated in soft pastels, silver wainscoting, and etched glass panels. Sleeping car accommodations were increased and included twenty-one duplex-roomettes, eighteen roomettes, twenty-four double bedrooms, nine compartments and nine compartment—double bedroom suite combinations. The last cars were beautifully appointed two-roomette/buffet/lounge/observation cars. These were named for mountains. An etched glass wall of western states' flowers separated the cars into two wood-paneled lounges with upholstered furnishings that could accommodate eighteen passengers each. The lounge cars had extra high windows to allow passengers to view the scenery along the line.

When the Mid-Century Empire Builder was introduced in June 1951, the Great Northern also inaugurated its companion streamliner—the

ABOVE: *The new streamlined Empire Builder passes the station at Glacier Park in 1948. The original E-7 locomotive is on the point. A freight is in the Glacier Park siding.*
COURTESY COLLECTION OF JOHN CHASE, GREAT FALLS, MT

LEFT: *Great Northern Railway timetable promoting the air conditioned Empire Builder. 1941.*
COURTESY JOHN CHASE COLLECTION AND BURLINGTON, NORTHERN, SANTA FE RAILWAY

GREAT NORTHERN RAILWAY

TIME TABLES

ROUTE OF THE
Air Conditioned
EMPIRE BUILDER

EFFECTIVE OCTOBER 15, 1941.

GLACIER NATIONAL PARK

Western Star, which was made with the four-year-old, still impressive equipment of the 1947 Empire Builder. It was the first double-daily streamliner service between Chicago and the Pacific and, for a time, the Great Northern lines enjoyed an increase in revenues.

Business and vacation travel by automobile was growing more popular despite the introduction of new, faster, more luxurious streamliner trains. In a last ditch effort to lure passengers back to railroad travel, the Great Northern debuted the Incomparable Great Dome Empire Builder in 1955. The Great Northern's dome cars were late coming on the line. The other railroads already offered dome cars on their scenic routes when the Great Dome Empire Builder debuted. The Great Northern, as was its practice when later than other railroads in adding a feature, went one better. Each of the five Empire Builders in service received three dome coaches and one full-length dome lounge car and 150 non-reserved dome seats available to standard-fare passengers—more, by far, than any other railroad offered.

Each dome coach had forty-eight reclining seats on the main level, which were reserved, and, upstairs, twenty-four lounge-type seats that were not reserved. The coaches were decorated in subdued colors with inlaid murals of Native American designs on interior walls. These all-glass observatories provided

MORE LUXURY DOME SEATS FOR THE MOST SCENIC

GO GREAT

4 GREAT DOMES ON T

Long a pacemaker for train travel at guished Empire Builder now provides 1 cars—the most dome seats on any strea Northwest cities.

There now are three luxurious Great Empire Builder . . . plus an exciting, co Pullman section, with America's smarte

For a vacation trip of a lifetime . . . f Empire Builder. There's *no extra fare fo* seat in the Great Domes for the *extra* Northern country.

For information: Write P. G. Holmes, Pass. T

panoramic views of the passing scenery.

The dome lounge cars featured a full-length dome area on the top deck with fifty-seven sofa seats angled for maximum viewing, and twenty-one lounge seats at the rear of the dome area. The lower deck provided a beverage bar, thirty-two sofa and lounge seats at tables, plus a writing desk and chair. The lounge car was decorated in a Western motif with multi-colored carvings and etched-glass totem pole panels. The lounges were given a view series name: Glacier View, Ocean View, Mountain View. The dome cars added to passengers' enjoyment as the scenery of the Northwest passed before them like a western movie, but even this latest innovation could not turn the tide of declining passenger traffic.

Despite all their investments to lure passengers aboard, the Great Northern faced the 1960s with rising costs and continuing declines in passenger traffic. The excitement and speed of commercial jet airplane travel and the convenience of the Interstate Highway System had won the transportation battle. In the first months of the 1960s, the Great Northern began implementing changes to its passenger train schedules and the *consists* of its Great Dome Empire Builder. Winter trains were significantly reduced, the Great Dome Lounge remained but the dome coach was removed, the number of sleepers was reduced and Day-Nite coach cars added.

In 1960, the National Governors Conference was held in Glacier National Park to commemorate the park's fiftieth anniversary. Although the Empire Builder had not stopped at Glacier since its inauguration as a transcontinental streamliner in 1947, "train-ordered" stops were made at the Glacier Park Station for the governors, their staffs, and the news media attending the conference at the Many Glacier Lodge. The Great Northern Board of Directors announced that it would continue to service the park during the summer season as long as travelers continued to travel on Great Northern trains to and from Glacier Park Station and Belton. At the same time they announced the potential sale of the Great Northern's hotels and lodges in the park.

LIKE THE SOUND OF AN OL' TIME FRIEND

By the 1970s, the northwestern United States' troubled railroads began a series of mergers. On March 3, 1970, the Great Northern, the Northern Pacific, and the Chicago, Burlington & Quincy merged to form the Burlington Northern Railway. A few months later, the Spokane, Portland & Seattle Railway was included, increasing the rail system of the new Burlington Northern to 24,398 miles. In 1980 the St. Louis–San Francisco Railway was added. The railway is now the Burlington-Northern-Santa Fe.

The Great Northern Empire Builder disappeared in the 1970 merger. However, Burlington Northern ran the train as the Empire Builder until the next year, when Amtrak took over the nation's passenger train service.

American rail travel had dropped steadily since its wartime high in 1944. Despite all that the railroads could do to reduce costs and lure passengers back to trains, the railroads had been losing an average of $525 million a year since the end of the war. The nation's passenger train service was about to go the way of the dinosaur when the National Railroad Passenger Corporation was formed in 1971 to operate a national rail-passenger system. It was financed by federal funding and loan guarantees, with about $200 million from the railroad compa-

BELOW: *Glacier Park ad for the 1960 Governors' Conference.*
COURTESY MR. LINDSAY KORST, GREAT NORTHERN RAILWAY HISTORICAL SOCIETY, WEBMASTER

Many Glacier Hotel area, headquarters for the 1960 Governors' Conference

Glacier National Park
Millions of years old – but celebrating its 50th birthday!

The Land of Shining Mountains . . . Montana's treasure of treasures . . . Glacier National Park is 50 years old this year.
This is an especially happy occasion for Great Northern Railway, which had an important role in the establishment of Glacier National Park.

Through these 50 years we have been host to legions of summer travelers in the lodges, hotels and motels of Glacier National Park—50 years of fun for visitors, and for us!
There's fun in store for you, too, in Glacier Park during its anniversary year. Go direct on Great Northern's Western Star.

Golden Anniversary Glacier National Park in Montana

For complete information on Glacier National Park vacations, including accommodations, costs and travel arrangements, write: P. G. HOLMES, Passenger Traffic Manager, Great Northern Railway, St. Paul 1, Minn.

nies that turned over their passenger service to the corporation. Passenger service of the Burlington Northern and most American railroads was turned over to the new corporation known as Amtrak (American travel by track). Amtrak preserved the nostalgic Empire Builder name on its train service between Chicago, St. Paul, and Seattle on the old Great Northern route and continues to serve Glacier National Park.

Early in the nineteenth century, leaders had predicted it would take 500 years to populate the west. By the turn of the twentieth century, five transcontinental railroads had bound the country together and the great American expansion was over. Railroads, for all their good and ill, helped unite the states and build the greatest economic power the world has ever known. They are not gone, they still clickity-clack singing to the railroad track through cities and towns and deserts and plains and mountains, but their golden years have slipped into history and, for many, into fond memory. The sight of a train rumbling by awakens our yearning for adventure; the mournful wail of the whistle reminds us of days gone by and days to come. It stirs our emotions as little else can. We try but can't explain that lump in our throats, the joy and the sadness we feel all at once when we hear that lonesome whistle blow. It's like the voice of an old time friend.

ABOVE: *Great Northern Railway brochure.*
COURTESY K. ROSS TOOLE ARCHIVES, UNIVERSITY OF MONTANA, MISSOULA

LEFT: *Oriental Limited, pulled by the famous first super heater used on passenger trains, crossing Cutbank Creek, 1913.*
COURTESY STUMPTOWN HISTORICAL SOCIETY, WHITEFISH, MT

BIBLIOGRAPHY

Atkinson, Gail Shay and Jim. *Izaak Walton Inn, A History of the Izaak Walton Inn and Essex, Montana.* Larry and Lynda Vielleux, Izaak Walton Inn, Essex, Montana. 1995.

Brown, Dee. *Hear That Lonesome Whistle Blow: Railroads of the West.* Holt, Rinehart and Winston, New York. 1977.

Djuff, Ray, and Chris Morrison. *Glacier's Historic Hotels & Chalets: View with a Room.* Farcountry Press, Helena, Montana. 2001.

Doyle, Theodore F. *Transcontinental GN Passenger Service.* Great Northern Historical Railway Society, St. Paul, Minnesota. 2000.

Flandrau, Grace. *The Story of Marias Pass.* Great Northern Railway, no date.

Grecula, Walt. *A Montana Story: History and Personal Perspectives.* Great Northern Railway Historical Society, St. Paul, Minnesota. 2003.

Holbrook, Stewart H. *James J. Hill: A Great Life in Brief,* Alfred A. Knopf, New York. 1955.

Middleton, Kenneth. *Early Great Northern Sleeping Cars.* Great Northern Railway Historical Society, St. Paul, Minnesota. 1996.

Peterka, Fr. Dale. *Early Steam Developments on the GN.* Great Northern Railway Historical Society, St. Paul, Minnesota. 1994.

Runte, Alfred. *Trains of Discovery: Western Railroads and the National Parks.* Northland Press, Flagstaff, Arizona. 1984.

Russell, Don, *Trails of the Iron Horse: An Informal History by The Western Writers of America.* Doubleday & Company, Inc., Garden City, New York. 1975.

Sayre, Walter. *Looking Back: Whimsical Whitefish Through the Years.* Stumptown Historical Society, Whitefish, Montana. 2003.

Schwantes, Carlos A. *Railroad Signatures Across the Pacific Northwest.* University of Washington Press, Seattle. 1993.

Tanner, Scott J. *A Biography of Winold Reiss: the man who created the Great Northern Railway's Blackfeet Indian portraits.* Great Northern Railway Historical Society, St. Paul, Minnesota. 1996.

Wheeler, Keith. *The Railroaders.* Time-Life Books, The Old West Series. Time Inc., New York. 1973.

Wood, Charles R. *Lines West, A Pictorial History of the Great Northern Railway Operations and Motive Power from 1887 to 1967.* Superior Publishing Company, Seattle, Washington. 1967

Yenne, Bill. *All Aboard! The Golden Age of American Rail Travel.* Brompton Books Corporation. 1989.

Great Northern Railway ink blotter.

AUTHOR BIOGRAPHY

C. W. Guthrie is a freelance writer living in the Ninemile Valley west of Missoula, Montana, with her husband retired test-pilot Joe Guthrie. She loves the mountains and valleys and history of Glacier National Park. This is her third book on the Park.

Index